Reyes-
Farsai

WORKBOOK

Principles of

Business, Marketing, and Finance

SECOND EDITION

Chris M. Gassen, MBA, CFA
Faircourt Valuation Investments
Grosse Pointe Woods, Michigan

Publisher
The Goodheart-Willcox Company, Inc.
Tinley Park, IL
www.g-w.com

The Goodheart-Willcox Company, Inc. Brand Disclaimer: Brand names, company names, and illustrations for products and services included in this text are provided for educational purposes only and do not represent or imply endorsement or recommendation by the author or the publisher.

The Goodheart-Willcox Company, Inc. Safety Notice: The reader is expressly advised to carefully read, understand, and apply all safety precautions and warnings described in this book or that might also be indicated in undertaking the activities and exercises described herein to minimize risk of personal injury or injury to others. Common sense and good judgment should also be exercised and applied to help avoid all potential hazards. The reader should always refer to the appropriate manufacturer's technical information, directions, and recommendations; then proceed with care to follow specific equipment operating instructions. The reader should understand these notices and cautions are not exhaustive.

The publisher makes no warranty or representation whatsoever, either expressed or implied, including but not limited to equipment, procedures, and applications described or referred to herein, their quality, performance, merchantability, or fitness for a particular purpose. The publisher assumes no responsibility for any changes, errors, or omissions in this book. The publisher specifically disclaims any liability whatsoever, including any direct, indirect, incidental, consequential, special, or exemplary damages resulting, in whole or in part, from the reader's use or reliance upon the information, instructions, procedures, warnings, cautions, applications, or other matter contained in this book. The publisher assumes no responsibility for the activities of the reader.

The Goodheart-Willcox Company, Inc. Internet Disclaimer: The Internet resources and listings in this Goodheart-Willcox Publisher product are provided solely as a convenience to you. These resources and listings were reviewed at the time of publication to provide you with accurate, safe, and appropriate information. Goodheart-Willcox Publisher has no control over the referenced websites and, due to the dynamic nature of the Internet, is not responsible or liable for the content, products, or performance of links to other websites or resources. Goodheart-Willcox Publisher makes no representation, either expressed or implied, regarding the content of these websites, and such references do not constitute an endorsement or recommendation of the information or content presented. It is your responsibility to take all protective measures to guard against inappropriate content, viruses, or other destructive elements.

Image Credits. Front cover: Band background: Tukang Desain/Shutterstock.com, Pipeline and people collage: Rawpixel.com/Shutterstock.com

Introduction

This workbook is designed for use with the *Principles of Business, Marketing, and Finance* textbook. As you complete the activities in this workbook, you will review the concepts, facts, and skills presented in the text. The activities in this workbook are divided into chapters that correspond to the chapters in the text. By reading the text first, you have the information needed to complete the activities.

Each chapter is organized into four parts: Content Review, Concept Review, Math Skills, and Communication Skills. The first two parts review the information presented in the textbook chapter and check your understanding of the concepts. The last two parts review math and communication skills necessary for college and career preparation and success.

The *Principles of Business, Marketing, and Finance* workbook is an effective self-assessment tool to prepare you for more formal assessment that your instructor may assign.

Table of Contents

Unit 6
Managing Your Career

Name _____ Date _____ Period _____

CHAPTER 1

Introduction to Business and Economics

Part 1: Content Review

Matching
Choose the letter of the correct term for each definition.

Terms:

A. economics
B. customer
C. cost-benefit analysis
D. scarcity
E. product

F. business
G. profit
H. capitalism
I. factors of production
J. service

1. _____ Process used to measure the benefits of a decision minus the costs associated with taking that action.

2. _____ Money that a business has left over after all the expenses and costs of running the business are paid.

3. _____ An economic system where the economic resources are privately owned by individuals rather than the government.

4. _____ Anything that can be bought and sold.

5. _____ When demand is higher than the available resources.

6. _____ An individual or group who buys products.

7. _____ An action or task that is performed, usually for a fee.

8. _____ A science that examines how goods and services are produced, sold, and used.

9. _____ The economic resources a nation uses to make goods and supply services for its population.

10. _____ A term for all the activities involved in developing and exchanging products.

Multiple Choice
Choose the letter of the correct answer to each question.

1. _____ Products are commonly known as _____.
   A. needs and wants
   B. goods and services
   C. factors of production
   D. functions of business

2. _____ Utility describes the characteristics of a product that satisfy _____.
   A. scarcity
   B. needs and wants
   C. opportunity costs
   D. supply and demand

3. _____ Which of the following is *not* a function of business?
   A. Capitalism
   B. Marketing
   C. Finance
   D. Production

4. _____ Entrepreneurs take risks to start and run _____.
   A. economic resources
   B. opportunity costs
   C. factors of production
   D. businesses

5. _____ The value of the next best option that is *not* selected is _____.
   A. profit
   B. standard of living
   C. opportunity cost
   D. time utility

6. _____ Which of the following is *not* an important economic question related to scarcity that every nation must answer?
   A. What should we produce?
   B. How should we produce it?
   C. For whom should we produce it?
   D. What are the factors of production?

7. _____ In a _____ economy, individuals are free to make their own economic decisions.
   A. market
   B. command
   C. centrally planned
   D. traditional

8. _____ The market price for a product is determined at a point where _____.
   A. demand exceeds supply
   B. supply exceeds demand
   C. supply equals demand
   D. there is both a shortage and surplus

9. _____ When demand for a product becomes greater than available supply, a(n) _____ develops.
   A. surplus
   B. shortage
   C. equilibrium
   D. competition

10. _____ The driving force in choosing to start a business is _____.
    A. supply and demand
    B. market forces
    C. competition
    D. profit

Completion

Choose the word(s) that best completes each of the following statements.

1. An individual or group that buys products is called a(n) _____.

   _____

2. A(n) _____ is something a person must have to survive.

   _____

3. _____ utility is added when products are available at convenient places.

_____

4. A(n) _____ is anywhere buyers and sellers meet to buy and sell goods and services.

_____

5. Money earned in exchange for work are _____.

_____

6. A business function that includes all business activities that involve money is _____.

_____

7. _____ is all of the tools, equipment, and machinery used to produce goods and services.

_____

8. A(n) _____ is when something is given up in order to gain something else.

_____

9. The government makes all the economic decisions for its citizens in a _____ economy.

_____

10. The price of product is determined by the law of _____.

_____

Part 2: Concept Review

Open Response
Respond to each of the following statements or questions. Use complete sentences.

1. What is a *customer*? Why must a successful business be focused on the customer?

_____

_____

_____

_____

_____

_____

_____

_____

_____

2. How do businesses generate economic benefits?

_____

_____

_____

_____

_____

_____

_____

_____

_____

_____

_____

3. What are *factors of production*? How do the factors of production relate to the basic economic problem?

_____

_____

_____

_____

_____

_____

_____

_____

_____

_____

Name _____

4. Identify and explain each of the functions of business.

   _____
   _____
   _____
   _____
   _____
   _____
   _____
   _____

5. In a mixed economy, both the government and individuals make decisions about economic resources. Think about how government is involved in the United States economy. Make a list of ten services provided by the federal, state, or local government. Indicate which you think are necessary for the country to function and survive. Briefly state your reasoning.

   _____
   _____
   _____
   _____
   _____
   _____
   _____
   _____
   _____
   _____
   _____
   _____
   _____

Part 3: Math Skills

Understanding Place Value

An understanding of *place value* is essential when working with numbers. Place value is the value of a digit based on its position in a number. Each place represents ten times the place to its right. This is a *base ten* system. The digit, or numeral, in the place farthest to the right *before* the decimal point is in the *ones position*. The next digit to the left is the *tens position*, followed by the next digit in the *hundreds position*. As you continue to move left, the place value increases to thousands, ten thousands, and so forth. The first digit which *follows* the decimal point to the right is in the *tenth position*, followed by the next digit in the *hundredth position*. As you continue to move right, the place values decrease to thousandths, ten thousandths, and so forth. The following figure demonstrates the numerical form of seven trillion, eight hundred sixty-three billion, one hundred fifty-nine million, two hundred thirty-seven thousand, five hundred eighty-four and one thousand eight hundred seventy-five ten thousandths.

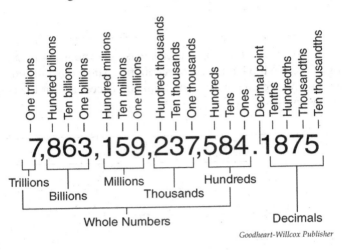

Goodheart-Willcox Publisher

Answer the following problems about place value.

1. A large corporation reports an annual profit at $375,000,000. How much is this profit in written form?

   _____

2. A business owner issues a paycheck in the amount of two thousand, three hundred fifty-seven dollars and forty-nine cents. What is the numerical amount of this check?

   _____

3. A business had sales last year of $139,526,000. Enter the value of the 9 digit in this number.

   _____

4. An employee earns wages of $69,243 this year compared to $54,357 last year. In which figure does the 4 digit have the larger value?

   _____

5. Consider the number $9,400.98. How many times greater is the nine on the left than the nine on the right?

   _____

Name _____

Part 4: Communication Skills

Writing

Communication skills are important in the workplace. To be an effective employee or employer, focus on improving your vocabulary so that you may become a skillful communicator. Vocabulary can be improved by understanding the difference between a synonym and an antonym. A *synonym* is a word that has the same meaning as another word. An *antonym* is a word that is the opposite of another word.

Section I

Choose the correct antonym from the following list to complete the sentences.

- early
- worst
- hot
- correct
- exit

- accept
- fast
- never
- clear
- open

1. Snowboards sell better when the weather is *cold*, while surfboards sell better when the weather is _____.
   _____

2. Customers were unhappy when the checkout lines were *slow*, and were happy when the lines moved _____.
   _____

3. The ice cream store was open *late* during July, but it closed _____ in January.
   _____

4. The teacher will *refuse* to accept a late assignment without an acceptable reason, but will _____ the assignment if an acceptable reason is given.
   _____

5. The customer service supervisor told employees to *always* be courteous, and _____ be rude.
   _____

6. The baseball team had its *best* attendance when the weather was sunny, but had the _____ attendance when the weather was rainy.
   _____

7. The salesclerk performed poorly when given *vague* directions, but performed well when the directions were _____.
   _____

8. The school office will be *closed* during the week of spring break, but will be _____ on the following Monday.
   _____

9. Employees must *enter* the headquarters building through the main doorway, and must _____ the building through the same door.
   _____

10. The *incorrect* response to a serious customer complaint is to argue with the customer, while the _____ response is to be calm and ask for a manager's assistance.
    _____

Section II

Next, choose an antonym for the following words.

11. Sad

_____

12. Build

_____

13. Rare

_____

14. Light

_____

15. Often

_____

16. Enemy

_____

17. Long

_____

18. Never

_____

19. Wrong

_____

20. Quiet

_____

21. Hot

_____

22. Public

_____

23. Sweet

_____

24. Strong

_____

25. Easy

_____

CHAPTER 2
Economic Activity

Part 1: Content Review

Matching
Choose the letter of the correct term for each definition.

Terms:

A. gross domestic product (GDP)   F. monopoly
B. inflation rate   G. fiscal policy
C. labor force   H. monetary policy
D. business cycle   I. commerce
E. recession   J. price fixing

1. _____ Central bank regulation of money supply and interest rates.

2. _____ Activities involved in buying and selling goods on a large scale.

3. _____ All the people in a nation who are capable of working and want to work.

4. _____ Occurs when two or more businesses in an industry agree to sell the same good or service at the same price.

5. _____ Alternating periods of expansion and contraction in an economy.

6. _____ Rate of change in prices calculated on a monthly or yearly basis.

7. _____ Tax and spending decisions made by the President and Congress.

8. _____ The market value of all final products produced in a country during a specific period of time.

9. _____ A period of significant decline in the total output, income, employment, and trade in an economy.

10. _____ Market structure with one business that has complete control of a market's entire supply of goods and services.

Multiple Choice
Choose the letter of the correct answer to each question.

1. _____ Gross domestic product (GDP) is also known as economic _____.
   A. input
   B. growth
   C. output
   D. policy

2. _____ Which type of spending is *not* a component of gross domestic product (GDP)?
   A. Consumer
   B. Business
   C. Government
   D. Stock market

3. _____ A general rise in prices throughout an economy is called _____.
   A. inflation
   B. deflation
   C. per capita GDP
   D. fiscal policy

4. _____ The amount a borrower pays for a loan is _____.
   A. lending
   B. interest
   C. inflation
   D. commerce

5. _____ A rising unemployment rates indicates a _____.
   A. stronger economy
   B. rising standard of living
   C. weaker economy
   D. period of hyperinflation

6. _____ Which is *not* a stage of the business cycle?
   A. Specialization
   B. Expansion
   C. Peak
   D. Recession

7. _____ A(n) _____ is a market structure with a small number of businesses selling the same or similar products.
   A. monopoly
   B. oligopoly
   C. monopolistic competition
   D. perfect competition

8. _____ Which of the following is *not* a role of government in an economy?
   A. Promote competition
   B. Provide a legal framework
   C. Promote monopolies
   D. Manage the economy

9. _____ Fiscal policy involves _____ decisions made by the government.
   A. tax and spending
   B. antitrust laws
   C. money supply and interest rates
   D. consumer protection

10. _____ The peak of a business cycle marks the _____.
    A. end of a contraction
    B. beginning of high unemployment
    C. end of an expansion
    D. beginning of government regulation

Completion

Choose the word(s) that best completes each of the following statements.

1. The strength of an economy can be measured using certain economic _____.

   _____

2. The economic growth rate of a country shows the amount and direction of the change in _____.

   _____

3. The activities involved in buying and selling goods on a large scale are considered _____.

   _____

4. The more products a worker produces in a given amount of time, the higher is the worker's _____.

_____

5. Ownership of a corporation is divided into _____.

_____

6. A period of economic contraction that is severe and lasts a long time is called a(n) _____.

_____

7. The central bank of the United States is the _____.

_____

8. Laws that promote fair trade and competition among businesses are known as _____ laws.

_____

9. Something that is *not* directly connected to economic activity, but that affects people, is called a(n) _____.

_____

10. A competitive advantage based on factors other than price is _____ competition.

_____

Part 2: Concept Review

Open Response

Respond to each of the following statements or questions. Use complete sentences.

1. Explain how gross domestic product (GDP) is used in making economic and business plans.

_____

_____

_____

_____

_____

_____

_____

_____

2. Explain the impact of high inflation on workers and consumers.

_____

_____

_____

_____

_____

_____

_____

_____

_____

_____

3. How might the government use monetary policies when the economy is slow or weak?

_____

_____

_____

_____

_____

_____

_____

_____

_____

Name _____

4. What are the four stages of the business cycle? Explain the activity in each stage.

_____
_____
_____
_____
_____
_____
_____
_____
_____
_____
_____

5. You are thinking about starting an athletic shoe company. Make a list of four factors or strategies you might use to gain an advantage over your competitors. Identify each as either a price or nonprice competition factor.

_____
_____
_____
_____
_____
_____
_____
_____
_____
_____
_____
_____
_____

Part 3: Math Skills

Order of Operations

The order of operations is a set of rules stating which operations in an equation are performed first. The order of operations is often stated using the acronym *PEMDAS*. PEMDAS stands for parentheses, exponents, multiplication and division, and addition and subtraction. This is the order in which computations are made.

It is important to follow this order so that the correct answer can be found. Take for example the following equation.

$$((45 \times 2) + (3 \times 7)^2 - 12) \div 2 =$$

According to PEMDAS, the equation is correctly solved by the following steps.

$$(45 \times 2) = 90$$
$$(3 \times 7) = 21$$
$$21^2 = 441$$
$$90 + 441 - 12 = 519$$
$$519 \div 2 = 259.5$$

If the equation is calculated by ignoring PEMDAS, the answer is incorrectly calculated as

$$((45 \times 2) + (3 \times 7)^2 - 12) \div 2 = 231$$

Use the order of operations to solve the following problems.

1. $13 \times (6 + 2) + 32 - 4 =$

_____

_____

_____

2. $12 \div (12 - 8) + 4 \times (8 - 2) - 3^2 =$

_____

_____

_____

3. $15 \times 4 + (19 - 17)^2 =$

_____

_____

_____

4. $((2 \times 7) + (4 \times 8) + (5 \times 11)) \div 101 =$

_____

_____

_____

5. $(10 + 2) + 2^2 \div (8 - 6) =$

_____

_____

_____

Part 4: Communication Skills

Listening

The ability to listen and process important information is an essential skill for any business owner or employee. It is difficult to properly follow instructions or serve a customer without listening carefully. Practice your listening skills. *Listen* carefully to a news story on television, radio, or an Internet stream. After the news report, answer the following questions.

1. Who: Who is the story about?

   _____

   _____

2. What: What is the main point of this story?

   _____

   _____

   _____

3. When: When did this story occur?

   _____

   _____

4. Where: Where did it occur?

   _____

   _____

5. Why: Why is this story important?

   _____

   _____

   _____

   _____

   _____

Notes

_____

CHAPTER 3 Business Law and Ethics

Part 1: Content Review

Matching

Choose the letter of the correct term for each definition.

Terms:

A. contract
B. lying
C. consideration
D. capacity
E. offer

F. ethics
G. confidentiality
H. morals
I. philanthropy
J. social responsibility

1. _____ A proposal to provide a good or service.

2. _____ An individual's ideas of what is right and wrong.

3. _____ Something of value promised in return for good or service.

4. _____ Making an untrue statement.

5. _____ Rules of behavior based on a group's ideas of what is right and wrong.

6. _____ Never sharing specific information about a company or its employees.

7. _____ Legally able to enter into a binding agreement.

8. _____ Behaving with sensitivity to social, environmental, and economic issues.

9. _____ A legally binding agreement between two or more people or businesses.

10. _____ Promoting the welfare of others.

Multiple Choice

Choose the letter of the correct answer to each question.

1. _____ Which of the following is *not* a required element of a contract?
   A. Offer
   B. Breach
   C. Acceptance
   D. Consideration

2. _____ Which is a contract used when two or more individuals create a business?
   A. Partnership agreement
   B. Lease
   C. Employment agreement
   D. Employment offer

3. _____ Which government agency works to prevent unfair competition and deceptive business practices?
   A. Consumer Product Safety Commission
   B. US Food and Drug Administration
   C. Federal Trade Commission
   D. US Department of Labor

4. _____ Businesses are required by federal law to give all workers _____.
   A. equal employment and advancement opportunities
   B. equal pay
   C. annual pay raises
   D. collective bargaining

5. _____ Environmental laws and regulations apply to _____.
   A. issues only relating to air and water pollution
   B. only companies with a certain number of employees
   C. problems related to worker compensation
   D. every type of business in every industry

6. _____ Businesses are expected to demonstrate ethical behavior _____.
   A. only when required by government regulation
   B. even when government regulations do not apply
   C. only when required by a contract
   D. except when it conflicts with corporate culture

7. _____ A company's code of conduct is likely to include rules on _____.
   A. hourly pay
   B. processes for handling outside contractors
   C. personal use of company Internet access
   D. signing a company confidentiality agreement

8. _____ _____ describes how the owners and employees think, feel, and act as a business.
   A. Social responsibility
   B. Corporate culture
   C. Philanthropy
   D. Integrity

9. _____ Principles that help define appropriate behavior in a business setting are _____.
   A. business ethics
   B. business regulations
   C. corporate culture
   D. morals

10. _____ Overstating the features and benefits of products is _____.
    A. a breach of confidentiality
    B. not subject to governmental regulations
    C. false advertising
    D. sometimes socially responsible

Completion

Choose the word(s) that best completes each of the following statements.

1. Each person who participates in a contract agreement is called a(n) _____.

   _____

2. Agreeing to the terms of a contract is _____.

   _____

3. Laws that apply to the handling of business debts when a business is no longer profitable are _____ laws.

   _____

4. The number assigned to businesses for tax purposes by the Internal Revenue Service (IRS) is a(n) _____.

   _____

5. _____ occurs when an employee uses proprietary information to purchase company stock or other securities for personal gain.

_____

6. The basic expectations of fair treatment of consumers are contained in the _____.

_____

7. A document that dictates how business should be conducted is a(n) _____.

_____

8. The honesty of a person's actions is called _____.

_____

9. Work created by company employees on the job that is owned by the company is _____.

_____

10. The actions taken by a business to promote social good are called _____.

_____

Part 2: Concept Review

Open Response

Respond to each of the following statements or questions. Use complete sentences.

1. Explain the importance of a contract in business.

   _____

   _____

   _____

   _____

   _____

   _____

   _____

2. Identify and briefly explain three types of business contracts.

   _____

   _____

   _____

   _____

   _____

   _____

   _____

   _____

   _____

3. What is a *code of ethics*? Explain its purpose in business.

   _____

   _____

   _____

   _____

   _____

   _____

   _____

4. Which government agency enforces fair employment practices laws? Explain how these regulations apply to businesses.

_____

_____

_____

_____

_____

_____

_____

5. You own a business that manufactures motor scooters. Create a chart listing two socially responsible actions your company can undertake in each of the following categories: environmental protection, employees and the workplace, consumer protection, and philanthropy.

_____

_____

_____

_____

_____

_____

_____

_____

Part 3: Math Skills

Whole Numbers, Decimals, and Fractions

Businesses buy and sell goods and services, for which there are prices. Prices in the United States are expressed in dollars and cents and can be whole numbers or decimals. A whole number is any positive number or zero that has no fractional part, such as $10, $25, or $100. A decimal is a kind of fraction with three parts: a whole number, followed by a decimal point, and one or more whole numbers. The numbers to the right of the decimal point indicate the amount of the fraction. The first place to the right of the decimal point is the tenths place; the second place to the right is the hundredths place. For example, a price of $12.59 would mean 12 dollars and 59 cents. Each cent is worth one hundredth of a dollar. Prices are sometimes reflected as decimals even when there are no cents. For example, $10 can also be written as $10.00.

Answer the following questions about prices.

1. Calculate the total amount of the following orders at an office supply store:

    Order #1

    Pens: $11.99

    Markers: $12.49

    Pencils: $3.99

    Total $ _____

    _____

    _____

    Order #2

    Printer: $139.00

    Laptop: $240.00

    Cables: $40.00

    Total $ _____

    _____

    _____

    Order #3

    Paper towels: $14

    Facial tissue: $11.50

    Hand soap: $11.25

    Total $ _____

    _____

    _____

2. A high school needs the following landscape supplies for its athletic field: fertilizer, seed, topsoil, and shovels. The school receives the following price quote from a local home and garden center.
    - Fertilizer $180
    - Seed $170
    - Topsoil $300
    - Shovels $75

    The home and garden center offers an additional $25 preseason discount and a $35 discount for not-for-profit organizations. How much is the high school's total bill?

    Total $ _____

    _____

    _____

Name _____

3. A pair of casual shoes is available at two online retailers: Shoe Mania and Walking Tall. The prices and shipping charges for each retailer are as follows. Calculate the total cost for each purchase. Which is less expensive?

Shoe Mania

Price: $129.99

Shipping charge: None

Total $ _____

_____

_____

Walking Tall

Price: $119.99

Shipping charge: $9.99

Total $ _____

_____

_____

4. You need a small electric motor for a science project. The prices and shipping charges from three online retailers are listed. In addition, there are coupons available for discounts. Calculate the total cost for each retailer. Which is the least expensive?

Elite Motor Supply

Price: $110

Shipping charge: None

Coupon: $5

Total $ _____

_____

_____

Electric.com

Price: $97.99

Shipping charge: $9.99

Coupon: None

Total $ _____

_____

_____

X-Way Devices

Price: $99.99

Shipping charge: $11.99

Coupon: $10

Total $ _____

_____

_____

5. You place the following food order at the Victory Veggie Deli: two black bean wraps, three organic pickles, bran chips, and two kale shakes. The following are the prices for each:
   - Bean wrap $6.50
   - Organic pickle $4
   - Bran chips $3.75
   - Kale shake $8.75

How much is the total order?

Total $ _____

_____

_____

Part 4: Communication Skills

Reading

Businesses must comply with a variety of legal requirements. Much of this information is communicated in documents that often use technical terms and phrases. When reading legal material, it is important to focus on understanding details. Read the following passage, focus on the content, and answer the questions.

Americans with Disabilities Act (ADA) Compliance

The Standard Axle Company (the Company) does *not* discriminate against qualified individuals with disabilities. This consists of every phase of the employment relationship, including the following:

- Recruitment, advertising, job applications, procedures
- Hiring, upgrading, promotion, demotion, transfer, termination, rehiring, and reinstatement
- Rates of pay or any other form of compensation and changes in compensation
- Job assignment, job classification, organizational structures, position descriptions, lines of progressions, seniority
- Leaves of absence, sick leaves
- Fringe benefits
- Selection and financial support for training, professional meetings, and seminars
- Company sponsored activities, including social and recreational programs
- Other terms, conditions, or privileges of employment

An individual has a disability when the person has a permanent physical or mental impairment that substantially limits one or more of the individual's major life activities, has a record of such impairment, or is regarded as having such impairment.

A "major life activity" is defined as an action that deals with the quality and necessity of life. Major life activities include, but are not limited to, actions related to the senses, such as seeing, hearing, and speaking as well as those dealing with day-to-day lifestyle activities, such as walking, eating, breathing, human reproduction, and working.

A qualified individual with a disability is anyone who satisfies the requisite skill, experience, education, and job-related requirements of the employment position and who can perform the essential functions of the job, with or without accommodation.

The Company complies with all aspects of the ADA and will provide reasonable accommodation to any individual deemed disabled under these regulations. The Company's goal is to assist disabled individuals in succeeding in their position. This will be done by ensuring they are given the same opportunities and held to the same standards and systems of behavior, and provided equal opportunity, incentive, and reward as any and all other team members. Specific accommodation requests will be reviewed and a determination made for each request on a case-by-case basis.

Reading Questions

1. Who is the author of this passage? Who is the intended audience?

   _____

   _____

   _____

   _____

2. What topic is discussed in this passage?

   _____

   _____

   _____

   _____

   _____

3. What are the conditions under which an individual is considered to have a disability?

_____

_____

_____

_____

_____

4. What is major life activity? What are some examples?

_____

_____

_____

_____

_____

5. What accommodations will the company make when requested by any individual deemed disabled under the ADA?

_____

_____

_____

_____

_____

CHAPTER 4

Business in the Free Enterprise

Part 1: Content Review

Matching
Choose the letter of the correct term for each definition.

Terms:

A. not-for-profit organization
B. producer
C. wholesaler
D. retailer
E. business market

F. proprietorship
G. stock
H. joint venture
I. cooperative
J. partnership

1. _____ A business that buys large quantities of products directly from producers and sells the products in smaller quantities to retailers.

2. _____ An association of two or more persons who co-own a business with the objective of earning a profit.

3. _____ A market that consists of customers who buy products for use in a business.

4. _____ A business that is owned and operated by those using its services.

5. _____ A business that buys products from wholesalers or directly from producers, and sells them to consumers to make a profit.

6. _____ A share of ownership in a corporation.

7. _____ An organization that exists to serve some public purpose.

8. _____ A business that is owned and often operated by a single individual.

9. _____ A business that creates goods and services.

10. _____ An agreement between two or more established organizations to pool their resources to achieve a specific goal.

Multiple Choice
Choose the letter of the correct answer to each question.

1. _____ Which of the following is an example of an intermediary?
   A. Auto manufacturer
   B. Auto parts manufacturer
   C. New car dealership
   D. Auto repair shop

2. _____ _____ is a numeric system to classify businesses and collect economic statistics.
   A. B2B
   B. NAICS
   C. LLC
   D. B2C

3. _____ Which is *not* an example of a not-for-profit organization?
    A. United Way
    B. American Cancer Society
    C. Microsoft
    D. American Red Cross

4. _____ An accounting firm that prepares taxes for an advertising agency operates in the _____ market.
    A. business-to-consumer
    B. consumer-to-business
    C. business-to-business
    D. consumer-to-consumer

5. _____ Which of the following is a business that is owned and operated by a single individual?
    A. Partnership
    B. Proprietorship
    C. Corporation
    D. Cooperative

6. _____ The two common types of partnerships are _____.
    A. general and unlimited
    B. general and cooperative
    C. general and limited
    D. limited and unlimited

7. _____ Which is *not* an advantage of a partnership form of ownership?
    A. Limited liability
    B. Easy to start
    C. Combined financial resources
    D. Simple tax structure

8. _____ Which is a form of business ownership provides limited liability to its owners, but is taxed as a partnership?
    A. S corporation
    B. Cooperative
    C. Green business
    D. Limited partnership

9. _____ A major advantage of forming a corporation is _____.
    A. profit
    B. limited life
    C. management
    D. limited liability

10. _____ Cooperatives are run _____.
    A. by the government
    B. democratically
    C. similarly to LLCs
    D. without voting members

Completion

Choose the word(s) that best completes each of the following statements.

1. One of the sole purposes of a for-profit business is to be productive and generate money for its _____.

_____

2. Governmental organizations are part of the _____ sector.

_____

3. The customer of a service business is often called a _____.

_____

4. The _____ market consists of customers who buy products for their own use.

_____

5. Wholesalers are often called _____.

_____

6. The simplest and most common form of business ownership is a(n) _____.

_____

7. A partner who does not participate in managing the business is a(n) _____ partner.

_____

8. The form of business ownership described as an "artificial person" is a(n) _____.

_____

9. The group of individuals who makes high-level management decisions for a corporation and establishes company policies is called the _____.

_____

10. The form of business ownership that combines the benefits of a corporation with those of proprietorships and partnerships is a(n) _____.

_____

Part 2: Concept Review

Open Response

Respond to each of the following statements or questions. Use complete sentences.

1. What is an intermediary? What benefit do they provide in business?

_____

_____

_____

_____

_____

2. What information should be detailed in the articles of partnership?

_____

_____

_____

_____

_____

3. What are the benefits and restrictions of an S corporation?

_____

_____

_____

_____

_____

_____

4. A disadvantage of proprietorships is unlimited liability. What is unlimited liability and why is it a disadvantage?

_____

_____

_____

_____

_____

_____

Name _____

5. A friend wants to start a business and asks your advice on the best form of ownership. Your friend is very smart and experienced, and prefers to make important decisions personally. Large sums of capital do not need to be raised, and the costs of forming the business are low. In addition, your friend has substantial personal wealth that will be kept separate from the business. Consider the following business forms: proprietorship, partnership, corporation, and limited liability company (LLC). Make a short argument for one of the forms of ownership for your friend.

_____

_____

_____

_____

_____

_____

_____

_____

Part 3: Math Skills

Word Problems

Basic math skills are essential to carry out the daily activities of a retail business. Real-life situations require that you understand how to interpret word problems. *Word problems* are exercises set up in text rather than presented with mathematical notation. There are two steps to solving a word problem. First, carefully read the problem and translate the wording into a numeric equation. Second, solve the equation.

Complete the following problems. Show the equation and solve the problem.

1. The free enterprise system is the driving force that enables retailers to make a profit and stay in business. Central Products is a manufacturer that generated sales of $838,515 last year. Total expenses were $719,311. What was the profit or loss last year?

_____

_____

2. Sigma Gears is a manufacturer that operates in the same industry as Central Products. Sigma's sales were $1,325,875 last year, with total expenses of $1,269,288. What was Sigma Gear's profit or loss? Compare Sigma Gear's profit or loss to Central Products in the previous question. Which company earned more money last year?

_____

_____

_____

3. The term *value-added* describes any enhancement to a good or service that makes consumers want to buy. Comparison shopping is a simple way to learn which product to buy and where to get the best value. You want to purchase a hot water heater. Ark Plumbing Supply has a model you like for $449. Jensen Warehouse, a competitor, sells the identical model for $599. Jensen offers free delivery, installation, and removal of your old heater. Ark Plumbing Supply charges $50 for delivery, $100 for installation, and $25 to remove the old heater. Which business offers the lower total purchase price?

_____

_____

_____

_____

4. Refer to the prices listed in the previous problem. You need a water heater and can install it yourself. You need delivery, but there is no old water heater to remove. Based on this information, at which business will you get the lower total price?

_____

_____

_____

_____

5. Ever-Brite Sponge Company manufactures various size sponges for household and janitorial use. The company sells its products to various retailers, as well as directly to the public through its website. Total sales last year were $800,000, of which $600,000 was to retailers.

   A. How much did Ever-Brite sell directly to the public?

_____

_____

B. Calculate the percentage of Ever-Brite's sales to the public using the following formula:

$$\frac{\text{sales to the public}}{\text{total sales}} \times 100 = \text{percentage of sales to the public}$$

_____

_____

Part 4: Communication Skills

Reading
Good reading skills are important in business. Read the following passage and focus on the content. Then, answer the questions that follow.

Diversity
Today, more than ever, companies benefit from employees with different backgrounds. Employees may differ in many ways: personality styles, education, age, gender, socioeconomic background, cultural background, race, religion, family situation, physical abilities, and lifestyles.

A diverse workforce is a reflection of a changing world and marketplace. The workforce of today and tomorrow is much more diverse than in the past. Bringing people from many backgrounds together in the workplace provides a greater diversity of talents, skills, ideas, and viewpoints. We welcome this diversity, as organizations that have a diverse workforce are most likely to thrive well into the future. However, a diverse workforce requires employees to work with coworkers of varied backgrounds. The Company must develop ways to maximize the potential of each employee.

A diverse workforce benefits the Company by creating a workplace where all employees have opportunities and feel good about their jobs. When employees' diversity is seen as an asset and employees are made to feel good about who they are and what they are capable of accomplishing, the Company can attract and retain good employees, maximize productivity, enhance the reputation of the Company, and improve decision making by having more viewpoints and choices.

A diverse workforce benefits employees because people are the happiest and most productive when they can be themselves. In a workplace that appreciates differences, people are valued as individuals and are not defined by stereotypes about their groups; employees are encouraged to discuss issues and resolve conflicts; employees acquire new skills through coaching, education, and shared knowledge among coworkers; and employees' needs and input are valued in developing job structures, work processes, conditions, and benefits.

The success of the Company is dependent upon the contributions of all its workers. In order to promote a fair and diverse workplace, employees must be respectful and open to others, especially when dealing with issues and people who may not always agree with their personal beliefs and values.

It is important to overcome bias and stereotypes. Every individual is unique and does not represent or speak for a group. Employees must talk to each other, hear each other, and work together for the success of the Company. Employees must recognize that they are interdependent and all must work together to accomplish goals.

Reading Questions

1. What is the main point of this passage?

   _____

   _____

   _____

   _____

   _____

   _____

   _____

Name _____

2. How does diversity benefit employees?

_____

_____

_____

_____

_____

_____

_____

3. Which paragraph of the passage explains how diversity benefits employers?

_____

_____

4. Upon what is the success of a company dependent?

_____

_____

_____

_____

_____

_____

_____

Notes

CHAPTER 5
Business in a Global Economy

Part 1: Content Review

Matching
Choose the letter of the correct term for each definition.

Terms:

A. globalization
B. exports
C. absolute advantage
D. balance of trade
E. tariff

F. logistics
G. licensing
H. franchise
I. quota
J. floating currency

1. _____ Goods and services produced within a country's borders and sold in another country.

2. _____ When a country can produce goods more efficiently and at a lower cost than another country.

3. _____ Planning and managing the flow of goods, services, and people to a destination.

4. _____ A limit on the amount of a product imported into a country during a specific period of time.

5. _____ When a business sells the right to manufacture its products or use its trademark.

6. _____ A governmental tax on imported goods.

7. _____ The connection among nations when economies freely move goods, labor, and money across borders.

8. _____ The right to sell a company's goods or services in a specific area.

9. _____ The difference between a nation's exports and its imports.

10. _____ The exchange rate is set by the forces of supply and demand in the foreign exchange market.

Multiple Choice
Choose the letter of the correct answer to each question.

1. _____ Which is *not* a benefit of exporting?
   A. Reduce legal documents
   B. Realize potential new markets
   C. Increase profits
   D. Generate jobs

2. _____ An absolute advantage exists when a country can produce goods more efficiently than _____.
   A. the previous year
   B. average
   C. with a floating currency
   D. another country

3. _____ Balance of trade is _____.
   A. exports plus imports
   B. exports minus imports
   C. exports minus tariffs
   D. the same as the balance of payments

4. _____ Most currencies today are _____.
   A. fixed
   B. restricted
   C. floating
   D. not influenced by economic factors

5. _____ Which of the following is *not* a trade barrier?
   A. Embargo
   B. Bloc
   C. Tariff
   D. Quota

6. _____ A group of countries that have reduced or eliminated trade barriers among themselves is a(n) _____.
   A. free-trade zone
   B. free-travel zone
   C. mutual trade area
   D. embargo zone

7. _____ The _____ for international shipping is more complex compared to domestic shipping.
   A. packaging
   B. logistics
   C. absolute advantage
   D. trade agreement

8. _____ Which of the following is *not* a business option to enter a foreign market?
   A. Licensing
   B. Franchising
   C. Comparative trade
   D. Joint venture

9. _____ The person or company that buys the rights to sell another company's goods or services in a specific area is a _____.
   A. franchise
   B. franchisor
   C. franchisee
   D. joint venture partner

10. _____ Someone who translates a conversation between individuals who do not speak the same language is a(n) _____.
    A. interrogator
    B. interloper
    C. interoffice liaison
    D. interpreter

Completion

Choose the word(s) that best completes each of the following statements.

1. _____ is the shared beliefs, customs, practice, and social behavior of a particular group or nation.

   _____

2. The buying and selling of goods and services across national borders is _____.

   _____

3. The total amount of money that comes into a country, minus the total amount of money that goes out for a specific period of time is the _____.

   _____

4. The cost to convert one currency into another is the _____.

_____

5. The body of laws related to the exchange of goods and services for international trade is called _____.

_____

6. An embargo that affects only certain goods is a(n) _____.

_____

7. The North American Free Trade Agreement (NAFTA) is a trade agreement that was replaced by _____.

_____

8. _____ is having people from different backgrounds, cultures, or demographics coming together in a group.

_____

9. The process of sending and receiving messages between people of various cultures is _____.

_____

10. A business that operates in more than one country is a _____.

_____

Part 2: Concept Review

Open Response

Respond to each of the following statements or questions. Use complete sentences.

1. What is exporting? List three advantages of exporting.

_____

_____

_____

_____

_____

_____

2. What is an absolute advantage? Why does it result in more global trade?

_____

_____

_____

_____

_____

_____

3. Most countries have their own currencies and typically only accept their own currency for business exchanges. How does this complicate global trade?

_____

_____

_____

_____

_____

_____

4. Give three reasons why countries impose trade restrictions on imports.

_____

_____

_____

_____

_____

_____

5. A company in Tulsa, Oklahoma wants to ship a 300 pound package to Takasaki, a city in Japan that is about 60 miles northeast of Tokyo. Think of two different ways to transport the package. Identify the methods of transportation involved in each. Which do you think would be faster? Which do you think would be more expensive?

_____

_____

_____

_____

_____

_____

_____

_____

_____

_____

Part 3: Math Skills

Conversions

The United States uses a system of measurement called the US Customary system. This system consists of feet, pounds, ounces, miles, inches, and degrees Fahrenheit. Most other countries use the *Système International d'Unités* (SI), or International System of Units, which consists of meters, grams, and degrees Celsius.

US Customary	SI
1 mile	1.60934 kilometer
3.28084 feet	1 meter
1 inch	2.54 centimeters
1 pound	453.592 grams
2.20462 pounds	1 kilogram
1 ounce	28.3495 grams

Goodheart-Willcox Publisher

Use the following equations to answer the questions involving conversions.

$$\text{degrees Celsius} = \frac{(\text{degrees Fahrenheit} - 32) \times 5}{9}$$

$$\text{degreen Fahrenheit} = \frac{\text{degrees Celsius} \times 9}{5} + 32$$

1. A delivery truck is traveling from Montana into Alberta, Canada. After crossing the border into Canada, the speed limit changes from miles per hour to kilometers per hour. The new speed limit is 125 kilometers per hour. If the truck is traveling at 75 miles per hour, is it under or over the speed limit?

_____

_____

2. A sporting goods company in Indiana receives an order to make soccer goals for a customer in Portugal. A regulation soccer goal is 24 feet wide and 8 feet high. What are the same dimensions in meters?

_____

_____

3. A medical products company in Atlanta receives an order from Spain for a special facial ointment. The standard package weight is 20 ounces. What is this weight in grams?

_____

_____

Name _____

4. A tourist is traveling back to the United States from Brazil and is checking baggage at the airport. The airline charges a $50 fee if a checked bag weighs over 50 pounds. The tourist checks a souvenir package that weighs 22 kilograms. Will the airline charge a fee?

_____

_____

_____

5. You hear the weather forecast on television in a Canadian hotel. The high temperature tomorrow will be 20 degrees Celsius. What is this temperature in degrees Fahrenheit?

_____

_____

_____

Part 4: Communication Skills

Speaking

Improving your vocabulary will help you as you communicate with a diverse group of customers. In the workplace, there are foreign expressions that you will encounter. Provide the definition for the following expressions.

1. De facto

   _____

2. Verboten

   _____

3. Carte blanche

   _____

4. Vis-à-vis

   _____

5. Status quo

   _____

6. Mea culpa

   _____

7. Mano a mano

   _____

8. Quid pro quo

   _____

9. Ad nauseum

   _____

10. Ex post facto

   _____

CHAPTER 6 Entrepreneurship

Part 1: Content Review

Matching

Choose the letter of the correct term for each definition.

Terms:

A. trait
B. leadership
C. mentor
D. market
E. cash flow

F. business plan
G. venture capital
H. capital structure
I. market research
J. start-up capital

1. _____ A written statement of goals and objectives for a business with a strategy to achieve them.

2. _____ The way a business is financed.

3. _____ The ability to influence others to reach a goal.

4. _____ The movement of money into and out of a business.

5. _____ A distinguishing characteristic or quality that makes each person unique.

6. _____ Gathering and analyzing information about a business.

7. _____ Someone with experience who can provide advice, suggestions, and ideas.

8. _____ The money necessary to start up and open a business.

9. _____ All the people and organizations that might purchase a product.

10. _____ Money invested in a business by investors who form partnerships or groups to pool investments.

Multiple Choice

Choose the letter of the correct answer to each question.

1. _____ Entrepreneurs willingly risk resources to start and run a business in pursuit of _____.
   A. planning
   B. profit
   C. pro forma
   D. professional advice

2. _____ Which of the following is a quality of effective leadership?
   A. Self-confidence
   B. Self-reliability
   C. Self-transferability
   D. Self-mentoring

3. _____ Which of the following is a basic skill every entrepreneur should master?
   A. Mentoring
   B. Basic math functions
   C. Franchising
   D. Angel investing

4. _____ Which of the following is a source of professional advice for new entrepreneurs?
   A. Federal Reserve System
   B. Small Business Administration (SBA)
   C. Federal Trade Commission (FTC)
   D. Food and Drug Administration (FDA)

5. _____ Which of the following is *not* a reason why many new businesses fail?
   A. Poor management skills
   B. Lack of money
   C. Lack of profit motive
   D. Improper budgeting

6. _____ An entrepreneur can choose to _____.
   A. start a new business
   B. purchase an existing business
   C. buy a franchise
   D. Any of the above.

7. _____ Which of the following is *not* a potential advantage of purchasing an existing business?
   A. History of profitable operations
   B. Proven products and sales strategies
   C. Expensive purchase price
   D. Guidance and advice from previous owner

8. _____ A business plan includes _____.
   A. financial projections
   B. approval from the Small Business Administration (SBA)
   C. approval from the Service Corps of Retired Executives (SCORE)
   D. collateral

9. _____ Which pro forma financial statement projects revenue and expenses to show whether or not a business is profitable?
   A. Balance sheet
   B. Cash flow statement
   C. Income tax return
   D. Income statement

10. _____ Two sources of equity financing are _____.
   A. angel investors and collateral
   B. venture capital and collateral
   C. venture capital and angel investors
   D. collateral and cash flow

Completion

Choose the word(s) that best completes each of the following statements.

1. A person who starts a new business or purchases an existing business is a(n) _____.

   _____

2. Entrepreneurs follow their _____, which is something they believe in or are enthusiastic about.

   _____

3. _____ skills help an individual perform in the workplace or gain success in a career.

   _____

4. An independent agency of the federal government dedicated to helping entrepreneurs start, build, and grow their business is the _____.

_____

5. A license to sell a company's goods or services within a certain territory or location is a(n) _____.

_____

6. A description of a business and why it will be successful is a(n) _____.

_____

7. A sentence describing the purpose of a business is a(n) _____.

_____

8. The _____ provides an overview of the industry and market that the business will serve.

_____

9. Property or items of value which a business owns are _____.

_____

10. Private investors who fund start-up businesses are _____.

_____

Part 2: Concept Review

Open Response

Respond to each of the following statements or questions. Use complete sentences.

1. Is a college degree needed to become an entrepreneur? Briefly explain your answer.

   _____

   _____

   _____

   _____

   _____

2. Why are problem-solving and decision-making skills essential to an entrepreneur?

   _____

   _____

   _____

   _____

   _____

3. What is the advantage of becoming an entrepreneur by buying a franchise?

   _____

   _____

   _____

   _____

   _____

4. Compare the advantages and disadvantages of debt financing and equity financing.

   _____

   _____

   _____

   _____

   _____

   _____

   _____

5. List and explain the five Ps of entrepreneurship.

_____

_____

_____

_____

_____

_____

_____

_____

_____

Part 3: Math Skills

Measurement of Area

The geometric principle of *area* is often applied when operating a business. Examples include planning for a store interior, advertising signage, or the layout for a work area. *Area* is a measure of the amount of surface within the perimeter of a flat figure. Area is measured in square units, such as square inches, square feet, or square miles. The following are formulas to calculate the area of a square and rectangular shaped surface:

Square: Side × Side
Rectangle: Length × Width

Answer the following questions involving area.

1. Trout Master Outdoors is a retailer that sells fishing and other outdoor recreation products. The owner wants to install wood flooring in a new section of the store that will display a new line of kayaks. This section is a square with 22 feet sides. How many square feet of wood flooring will be needed?

   _____

   _____

2. A sports and concert arena wants to install a giant LED billboard on a nearby highway to advertise upcoming events. The billboard is 48 feet high and 80 feet long. The general manager of the arena discovers there is local ordinance that limits the area of any outdoor signage to 3,000 square feet. Will this video display meet the ordinance requirements?

   _____

   _____

3. Premier Design Company is leasing a building for a new engineering research department. The space is 70 feet long and 60 feet wide. The office and reception area will use 15 percent of the space. How many square feet will be used for the office and reception area?

   _____

   _____

4. Argosy Corporation needs 30 more parking spots for its employees. Next to its headquarters building, there is vacant land that is 200 feet long and 70 feet wide. When building a parking lot, 350 square feet is needed for each parking spot. Will this land be large enough for 30 more parking spots?

   _____

   _____

5. A high school wants to install new turf on its football field. The football field is regulation size at 120 yards long and 53.33 yards wide. How many square yards of turf are needed?

   _____

   _____

Part 4: Communication Skills

Reading

Reading for information is much different than reading for pleasure. When reading for information, be sure to ask yourself questions about what you have read to ensure understanding. Read the passage below and focus on the content. After you have read the passage, answer the questions that follow.

Developing a Mentoring Relationship

In life and in business, mentoring relationships develop when a veteran professional takes on the responsibility of serving as a role model for a younger person or for a new employee. Veteran professionals may not realize the leadership skills they pass on to young people or the influence they have by serving as mentors. Barnes, Mendleson, and Horn (1989) defined mentoring as "an older, wiser advisor serving as a role model and guide in the growth and development of the younger persons."

Thinking Positively

Expectations of young people are important in their growth and success. Veteran employees communicate both high and low expectations to young or newer employees and do so through both verbal and nonverbal behaviors. Young people learn to think positively and use these ten winning two-letter words: "if it is to be, it is up to me." Veteran employees or managers should encourage young or newer employees to set obtainable goals, plan their programs of work, document their career and life objectives, and associate with winners, not losers. Young people should write their 'wins' down for future reference. Many attorneys have special files of all of their 'win' cases and their 'lost' cases and use these files to guide their future endeavors. Others can develop a similar filing agenda.

Listening and Observing

An employer may tell new employees, "Keep your eyes and ears open and your mouths shut for the first few weeks you are here. You will learn a great deal more about us that way." Mentoring in business has been rediscovered, so to speak, as more workshops and seminars are being offered for training (Hannah 2009).

Leaders should not be expected to have all the answers; thus, they must listen to their followers and other advisors to learn new directions and solutions to problems.

Sources:
Hannah, Daryl C. "How to Build a Successful Mentorship," *DiversityInc*, February 13, 2009.
Mendleson, Jack L., A. Keith Barnes, and Gregory Horn. "The Guiding Light to Corporate Culture," *Personnel Administrator*, July 1989: 70+. *General OneFile*, accessed December 16, 2010.

Reading Questions

1. What is a mentor?

_____

_____

_____

_____

_____

2. What are the ten winning two-letter words?

_____

_____

_____

3. What should veteran employees and managers encourage younger employees to do?

_____

_____

_____

_____

_____

_____

Name _____ Date _____ Period _____

Business Organization, Management, and Leadership

Part 1: Content Review

Matching
Choose the letter of the correct term for each definition.

Terms:

A. goal

B. procedure

C. staffing

D. controlling

E. management

F. communication skills

G. compromise

H. teamwork

I. negotiation

J. mediation

1. _____ To give up an individual idea, or part of an idea, so that the group can come to a solution.

2. _____ Cooperative efforts by individual team members to achieve a goal.

3. _____ The process of controlling and making decisions about a business.

4. _____ When individuals involved in a conflict come together to discuss a compromise.

5. _____ Something to be achieved in a specified period of time.

6. _____ The process of recruiting, hiring, training, evaluating, and compensating employees.

7. _____ Helps people communicate and work well with each other.

8. _____ A continuous process of evaluating the progress in reaching goals and making corrections to plans, when necessary.

9. _____ Process in which a neutral person meets with each side of a negotiation in an attempt to find a solution that both sides will accept.

10. _____ Describes how tasks should be completed.

Multiple Choice
Choose the letter of the correct answer to each question.

1. _____ Something to be achieved in a specified period of time, generally less than a year, is a _____.
   A. plan
   B. short-term goal
   C. long-term goal
   D. procedure

2. _____ An operating guide for using equipment is an example of a(n) _____.
   A. procedure
   B. objective
   C. goal
   D. organization chart

3. _____ _____ is when all the authority within a business rests with top management.
   A. Departmentalization
   B. Middle management
   C. Decentralized organization
   D. Centralized organization

4. _____ A foreman or shift manager is considered _____ management.
   A. middle
   B. first-line
   C. top
   D. organizational

5. _____ Which is *not* a type of management plan?
   A. Strategic
   B. Tactical
   C. Procedural
   D. Contingency

6. _____ Which of the following is an example of a leadership style?
   A. Automatic
   B. Academic
   C. Democratic
   D. Realistic

7. _____ _____ skills are the ability to analyze a situation, interpret information, and make reasonable decisions.
   A. Critical-thinking
   B. Verbal
   C. Collaboration
   D. Listening

8. _____ Expressing individual needs with little interest in or respect to the needs of others is _____ behavior.
   A. aggressive
   B. assertive
   C. passive
   D. creative

9. _____ The process of recognizing and resolving team disputes in a balanced and effective way is _____.
   A. teambuilding
   B. procedural guidance
   C. middle management
   D. conflict management

10. _____ Interactive forces within a group are known as _____.
    A. brainstorming
    B. compromising
    C. group dynamics
    D. mediating

Completion

Choose the word(s) that best completes each of the following statements.

1. Effective businesses establish guidelines for their organization which are sometimes called _____.

_____

2. A sentence that describes the purpose of a company and why it exists is a(n) _____.

_____

3. The _____ of a business identifies the hierarchy of the employees within the business.

_____

4. A diagram that shows the structure of an organization is a(n) _____.

_____

5. A(n) _____ organization is when authority within a business is given to various managers that run their own department.

_____

6. _____ management consists of a company's board of directors, president, and other high-ranking managers.

_____

7. The process of recruiting, hiring, training, evaluating, and compensating employees is _____.

_____

8. A hands-off approach to leadership is a(n) _____ style.

_____

9. A(n) _____ system is used to acquire, organize, maintain, retrieve, and use information.

_____

10. A(n) _____ goal is one that is specific, measurable, attainable, realistic, and timely.

_____

Chapter 7   Business Organization, Management, and Leadership   55

Part 2: Concept Review

Open Response

Respond to each of the following statements or questions. Use complete sentences.

1. What are the five functions of management? Briefly describe each function.

    _____

    _____

    _____

    _____

    _____

    _____

    _____

2. Compare the typical responsibilities of middle management positions and first-line managers.

    _____

    _____

    _____

    _____

    _____

    _____

    _____

3. What are communication skills? Give three examples of important communication skills and explain how each helps a leader to be effective.

    _____

    _____

    _____

    _____

    _____

    _____

    _____

Name _____

4. What are the common steps in a conflict-resolution model?

_____

_____

_____

_____

_____

_____

_____

5. Think of a business you would like to start. Write a simple, one-sentence mission statement for this company. Then, expand the mission statement to be more detailed.

_____

_____

_____

_____

_____

_____

Part 3: Math Skills

Mixed Mathematics

Management is responsible for the success of a business. Some larger businesses have multiple stores, divisions, or subsidiaries with mangers that are in charge of each. Business owners often create goals that each of their managers must meet. It is then the responsibility of each manager to execute the plans and meet these goals. Performance is then measured to determine if success is being achieved. One way to measure performance is with numerical or quantitative standards called *metrics*. Two popular metrics are profit and profit/assets. Profit metrics measure the amount of profit earned by the manager of each store, division, or subsidiary. This is simply sales minus expenses:

$$sales - expenses = profit$$

Profit/assets metrics measure the amount of profit earned in relation to the amount of assets that are invested. It is often expressed as a percentage and is sometimes called the *return on assets*.

$$\frac{profit}{total\ assets} = return\ on\ assets,\ or\ profit/assets$$

To convert a value to a percent, move the decimal point two places to the right.
Answer the following questions involving performance metrics.

1. Creative Crafts is a specialty retailer of art and craft supplies with two stores. Performance metrics for the entire business last year are as follows:

   Total Sales: $350,000

   Total Expenses: $247,000

   Total Assets: $630,000

   A. Calculate the profit for this business.

   _____

   _____

   B. Calculate the profit/assets percentage for this business.

   _____

   _____

2. The following shows the total performance data of Creative Crafts divided between its two stores. Store #1 is larger than Store #2 and has more invested in assets for the building, store fixtures, and inventory.

   Store #1:

   Total Sales: $200,000

   Total Expenses: $145,000

   Total Assets: $380,000

   Store #2

   Total Sales: $150,000

   Total Expenses: $102,000

   Total Assets: $250,000

   A. Calculate the profit for Store #1.

   _____

   _____

   B. Calculate the profit/assets percentage for Store #1.

   _____

   _____

C. Calculate the profit for Store #2.

_____

_____

D. Calculate the profit/assets percentage for Store #2.

_____

_____

3. Refer to data in the previous problem. The manager of Store #1 believes the store is performing better than Store #2 because Store #1's profits are greater. Is this correct? Support your opinion with performance metrics.

_____

_____

_____

_____

_____

_____

4. Dog Bonz manufactures rawhide bones for dogs. Net sales last year were $610,000 and expenses were $440,000. Assets in the company total $1,900,000. Calculate the following metrics.

A. Calculate the profit for Dog Bonz.

_____

_____

B. Calculate the profit/assets percentage for Dog Bonz.

_____

_____

5. The owner of Dog Bonz considers starting a new and separate division to make dog toys. This new division will require an investment in assets totaling $800,000. Sales are expected to be $420,000, with projected expenses of $390,000.

A. Calculate the expected profit for the new dog toy division.

_____

_____

B. Calculate the profit/assets percentage for the new dog toy division.

_____

_____

C. How does the profit/assets metric of this new division compare to the existing business?

_____

_____

_____

Part 4: Communication Skills

Reading

Reading skills are essential in business. Imagine the potential problems if someone misreads the terms of a contract or purchase order. The ability to read through text and determine important information is a skill employers look for when hiring. Read the passage below and focus on the content. After you have read the passage, write the answers to the activities that follow.

Workplace Privacy

The ABC Company provides communication services and equipment necessary to promote the efficient conduct of Company business. All business equipment, electronic and telephone communications systems, and all communications and stored information transmitted, received, or contained in the Company's information systems are the Company's property and no expectation of privacy regarding these communications and business equipment should be assumed. To ensure the proper use of communications systems and business equipment, the Company may monitor the use of these systems and equipment and review or inspect all material stored therein from time to time. No communications are guaranteed to be private or confidential.

Software and Business Equipment

The Company discourages personal, nonbusiness-related use of its software and business equipment, including, but not limited to, computers, copy machines, and digital scanners. Employees are prohibited from using codes, accessing files, or retrieving any stored communications without prior authorization from the appropriate supervisor or the Information Technology Department.

Employees must be aware of the possibility that electronic messages believed to have been erased or deleted can frequently be retrieved by systems experts and can be used against an employee or the Company. Therefore, employees should be cautious and use the systems only in the appropriate manner and consult with the Information Technology Department to guarantee that information deleted is truly eliminated from the system.

Passwords

No employee may use a password unknown to the Company. The use of passwords assigned to the employee is *not* grounds for an employee to claim privacy rights in the electronic or communications systems. The Company reserves the right to override personal passwords. Employees may be required to disclose passwords or codes to the Company to allow access to the systems.

Photographs and Video and Voice Recordings

No employee may take a photo or make a recording of any type of coworkers or business associates without the subject's knowledge. No employee may take photos or make a recording of any type of Company property or proprietary information without permission of the Company president.

Use of Copyrighted Materials

Employees are prohibited from disseminating, printing, or copying copyrighted materials or in any other way violating copyright laws. The electronic posting of copyrighted information is also prohibited, unless the Company or an employee created the information or owns the rights to it.

Reading Questions

1. What is the policy concerning video and voice recordings?

_____

_____

_____

_____

_____

Name _____

2. Are ABC employees prohibited from any personal, nonbusiness use of software and business equipment?

_____

_____

_____

_____

3. Why do you think that employers issue policies about workplace privacy?

_____

_____

_____

_____

_____

_____

Notes

CHAPTER 8   Production of Goods

Part 1: Content Review

Matching
Choose the letter of the correct term for each definition.

Terms:

A. conversion
B. sourcing
C. mass production
D. supplier
E. inventory

F. repositioning
G. image
H. prototype
I. test marketing
J. product planning

1. _____ The process of deciding which products will be most strategic for the organization to produce.

2. _____ Marketing an existing product in a new way to create a new opinion or view of the product in the minds of customers to increase sales.

3. _____ The assortment or selection of items that a business has on hand at a particular point in time.

4. _____ A working model of a new product for testing purposes.

5. _____ The process of changing and improving resources to create goods or services.

6. _____ Finding suppliers of materials needed for production of a product.

7. _____ The idea that people have about someone or something.

8. _____ Manufacturing goods in large quantities using standard techniques.

9. _____ Business that sells materials, supplies, or services to an organization that creates product.

10. _____ Introduction of a new product to a small portion of the target market to learn how it will sell.

Multiple Choice
Choose the letter of the correct answer to each question.

1. _____ _____ utility is important in production because it includes the conversion of raw materials into finished product.
   A. Time
   B. Place
   C. Possession
   D. Form

2. _____ The specialization of individuals who perform specific tasks is _____.
   A. mass production
   B. division of labor
   C. productivity
   D. custom manufacturing

3. _____ Which is *not* a typical activity in an effective production process?
   A. Planning
   B. Purchasing
   C. Repositioning
   D. Scheduling

4. _____ A _____ inventory control system keeps a minimal amount of raw materials on hand to meet production needs.
   A. just-in-time
   B. right-on-time
   C. periodic
   D. continuous

5. _____ The activity of checking products as they are produced or received to ensure quality meets expectations is _____.
   A. inventory control
   B. quality control
   C. just-in-time
   D. continuous process improvement

6. _____ _____ is the series of stages a product goes through from its beginning to its end.
   A. Repackaging
   B. Repositioning
   C. Test marketing
   D. Product life cycle

7. _____ In the new product development process, a new product is introduced to the market during the _____ stage.
   A. commercialization
   B. evaluation
   C. idea screening
   D. business analysis

8. _____ Testing new services before they are commercially available is accomplished through _____.
   A. surveys
   B. trade shows
   C. trial runs
   D. evaluation

9. _____ Introducing a new product to a small portion of the target market to learn how it will sell is _____.
   A. test marketing
   B. a prototype
   C. idea screening
   D. branding

10. _____ Using a new package for an existing product is _____.
   A. repositioning
   B. repackaging
   C. realignment
   D. redesigning

Completion

Choose the word(s) that best completes each of the following statements.

1. The area of management responsible for the activities necessary to produce goods and services is _____.

   _____

2. _____ describes the characteristics of a product that satisfy wants and needs.

   _____

3. The measure of a worker's production in a specific amount of time is _____.

_____

4. Converting resources to a product that fits the specifications of a particular customer is _____.

_____

5. The _____ is all the activities required to create a product.

_____

6. _____ inventory consists of products that are partially converted.

_____

7. A(n) _____ inventory-control system is a method of counting inventory that shows the quantity on hand at all times.

_____

8. The difference between the perpetual inventory and the physical inventory is _____.

_____

9. A working model of a new product for testing purposes is a(n) _____.

_____

10. A large gathering of businesses for the purpose of displaying goods and services for sale is a(n) _____.

_____

Part 2: Concept Review

Open Response

Respond to each of the following statements or questions. Use complete sentences.

1. What is productivity? How can productivity be improved?

_____

_____

_____

_____

_____

_____

_____

2. What is inventory management? What is the risk in carrying too much inventory? What is the risk in carrying too little inventory?

_____

_____

_____

_____

_____

_____

_____

_____

3. What is inventory shrinkage? Explain the main causes of inventory shrinkage.

_____

_____

_____

_____

_____

_____

_____

_____

4. What is the product life cycle? Identify three strategies to address a product that is at the end of its life cycle.

_____

_____

_____

_____

_____

_____

_____

5. Do you think the product life cycle is the same length for every product? Compare the life cycle of two products: Quaker Oatmeal and VHS movie tapes. Which product life cycle has been longer? Think of at least two ways Quaker has tried to lengthen the life cycle of its product over the years.

_____

_____

_____

_____

_____

_____

_____

_____

_____

_____

_____

Part 3: Math Skills

Estimating

Sometimes it is more practical to estimate the answer to a math problem than to calculate it precisely. Precision is not always needed and estimating is easier. *Estimation* is a process of finding an approximate answer. It often involves using rounded numbers, which are easier to work with than precise numbers. Businesses often use estimates in their daily work.

Answer the following problems by using rounded numbers and estimating.

1. Henson Classic Cars in Detroit, Michigan sells classic and collectible automobiles. The company makes its own deliveries and pickups to ensure that its cars are not damaged. One of Henson's delivery vehicles will travel to Chicago, then to St. Louis, and finally to Wichita. The following is the mileage for each segment of the trip.
   - Detroit to Chicago: 289 miles
   - Chicago to St. Louis: 314 miles
   - St. Louis to Wichita: 438 miles

   Estimate the total mileage for three segments of the trip.

   _____

   _____

   _____

2. Gleason Fabrication Company manufactures specialty fasteners for building constructors. A purchasing manager at Gleason places raw material orders with the following vendors.
   - Sentry Steel $11,755
   - C&P Metals $29,211
   - Granger Parts $20,613
   - Garret Cutters $14,765

   The current purchase limit is $70,000. Estimate if the total amount of the four purchases will exceed the limit.

   _____

   _____

   _____

3. Sales last week at Downtown Diner were $4,814. If sales during most weeks are approximately the same, estimate the monthly sales for Downtown Diner based on these weekly results.

   _____

   _____

   _____

4. Comfort Heating & Cooling sells and services home furnaces and air conditioners. A customer calls and asks for a "ballpark" price on a XL-500 Gas Furnace with a TBR-950 electronic air filter. The gas furnace is priced at $2,799 and the air filter sells for $569. Give the customer an approximate price.

   _____

   _____

   _____

5. An apartment owner needs new carpet. The apartment size is 935 square feet. A local carpet store will install carpet and padding for $1.85 a square foot. Approximately what will the new carpet cost?

   _____

   _____

   _____

Part 4: Communication Skills

Writing

Developing proper writing skills is important in effectively communicating with others. Edit the following paragraph. Insert proper punctuation, correct misspelled words and grammar errors, and rewrite sentences to improve the structure, as needed.

each november we close the ware house for ten business days to take our annual inventorey. this year, we will close from monday november 4, threw friday november 15. as always we will notify all customers by enclosing a flier with they're october statements. we also notify all our employes so the warehouse closing does not adversely effect business operations so if you need any supplies or products we urge you to note the above dates and submit your requisitions as early as possible to avoid the end-of-october rush. please try to anticipate your needs as best you can.

Notes

CHAPTER 9 Human Resources Management

Part 1: Content Review

Matching

Choose the letter of the correct term for each definition.

Terms:

A. human resources
B. job description
C. inclusion
D. commission
E. diversity

F. benefit
G. flextime
H. discrimination
I. harassment
J. telecommuting

1. _____ Having representatives from different backgrounds, cultures, or demographics in a group.

2. _____ The employees who work for a business.

3. _____ An arrangement where employees work away from the business site.

4. _____ A policy allowing employees to adjust work schedules to better match personal schedules.

5. _____ When an individual is treated unfairly because of race, gender, religion, national origin, disability, or age.

6. _____ Defines the position and expectation for a job.

7. _____ The practice of recognizing, accepting, and respecting diversity.

8. _____ Uninvited conduct toward a person based on race, color, religion, sex, national origin, age, or disability.

9. _____ A form of noncash compensation received in addition to a wage or salary.

10. _____ Income paid as a percentage of sales made by a salesperson.

Multiple Choice

Choose the letter of the correct answer to each question.

1. _____ Which of the following is *not* a human resources management function?
   A. Recruiting and hiring
   B. Training and development
   C. Compensation
   D. Scheduling resources

2. _____ Recruiting and hiring involves which of the following functions?
   A. Conducting interviews
   B. Job-specific training
   C. Professional development
   D. Arbitration

3. _____ Which of the following would *not* be considered an employee benefit?
   A. Medical insurance
   B. Childcare
   C. Salary
   D. Retirement plan

4. _____ Incentives are a type of compensation based on _____.
   A. age
   B. performance
   C. tax bracket
   D. ergonomics

5. _____ A formal negotiation process between management and unions to resolve issues is called _____.
   A. collective bargaining
   B. strike
   C. mediation
   D. arbitration

6. _____ The most common laws affecting human resources management involve _____.
   A. fair and equal treatment and working conditions
   B. training and development
   C. performance evaluation
   D. job analysis

7. _____ _____ is one way an organization may offer employees the ability to balance job and family life responsibilities.
   A. Vacation time
   B. Mutual reliance
   C. Overtime
   D. Telecommuting

8. _____ According to Maslow's Hierarchy of Needs, needs motivate _____.
   A. tax allowances
   B. people to act
   C. people to strike
   D. legal compliance

9. _____ A common characteristic of effective employer/employee relationships is mutual _____.
   A. training
   B. arbitration
   C. respect
   D. orientation

10. _____ Which of the following would involve ergonomics?
    A. More visible safety signs
    B. Better compensation
    C. Mutual reliance
    D. Comfortable computer stations

Completion

Choose the word(s) that best completes each of the following statements.

1. A(n) _____ is a process that identifies the job requirements for a position, employee qualifications, and how success will be evaluated.

   _____

2. The strategy used to find people who are qualified for a position is _____.

   _____

3. Education for people who have already completed their formal schooling and training is _____.

   _____

4. Payment for work that is usually calculated on a hourly, daily, or weekly basis is called _____.

   _____

5. A wage based on a rate per unit of work completed is _____.

_____

6. A general reduction in the number of employees within a company is _____.

_____

7. A group of workers united as a single body to protect and advance the rights and interests of its members is a(n) _____.

_____

8. Time off from work designated for certain life events is _____.

_____

9. Any action that denies opportunities, privileges, or rewards based on a person's gender is called _____.

_____

10. The term _____ describes how the owners and employees of a company think, feel, and act as a business.

_____

Part 2: Concept Review

Open Response

Respond to each of the following statements or questions. Use complete sentences.

1. What is a job application form? What information is typically included on this form?

_____

_____

_____

_____

_____

2. Describe the role of human resources management (HRM) for a business or organization.

_____

_____

_____

_____

_____

3. Describe the HRM function of legal compliance. What are some areas of HR laws and policies?

_____

_____

_____

_____

_____

4. What is the motivation/hygiene theory? Explain how this relates to corporate culture.

_____

_____

_____

_____

_____

_____

_____

Name _____

5. Many US laws describe the proper treatment expected for employees in the workplace. Explain the difference between discrimination and harassment in the workplace.

_____

_____

_____

_____

_____

_____

_____

_____

Part 3: Math Skills

Multiplication

Math is an integral part of a businessperson's skill set. One of the most commonly used math applications is multiplication. Multiplication is a method of adding a number to itself a given number of times. The multiplied numbers are called *factors*, and the result is called the *product*. For example, suppose you want to purchase five pens that cost $3 each. The total cost can be found by adding $3 five times:

$$\$3 + \$3 + \$3 + \$3 + \$3 = \$15$$

However, the same answer is found more quickly by multiplying $3 times 5:

$$\$3 \times 5 = \$15$$

To multiply decimals, place the numbers in a vertical list. Then multiply each digit of the top number by the right-hand bottom number. Multiply each digit of the top number by the bottom number in the tens position. Place the result on a second line and add a zero to the end of the number. Add those two lines together to find your answer. Finally, add the total number of decimal places in both numbers you are multiplying. This will be the number of decimal places in your answer. For example, suppose you buy 12 notebooks which cost $2.60 each. The total cost is found by multiplying $2.60 by 12:

$$
\begin{array}{r}
\$2.60 \\
\times\ 12 \\
\hline
520 \\
+\ 2600 \\
\hline
\$31.20
\end{array}
$$

Answer the following multiplication problems.

1. You buy six tickets to a local music festival at $29.85 each. What is the total cost?

   _____

   _____

2. Refer to the previous problem. The music festival is running a special promotion. If you buy at least a dozen tickets, the price is only $24.95 each. You buy 12 tickets.

   A. What is the total cost?

   _____

   B. How much more does it cost to double your purchase from 6 to 12 tickets?

   _____

   _____

3. Pet Express receives an order for four cases of large chew sticks. There are 24 sticks in a case and each chew stick is priced at $3.20. What is the total cost of the order?

   _____

   _____

   _____

4. Pet Express receives an order for three different sizes of Maxi Fresh Cat Litter. Calculate the order cost for each of the following sizes:

   A. 8 pound bag

      Cost: $9.25

      Number ordered: 8

_____

_____

   B. 12 pound bag

      Cost: $12.25

      Number ordered: 12

_____

_____

   C. 20 pound bag

      Cost: $19.75

      Number ordered: 18

_____

_____

   D. What is the total amount of this order?

_____

_____

5. Yard Master receives an order for 11 backyard fence kits priced at $129.99 each. What is the total cost of the order?

_____

_____

Part 4: Communication Skills

Reading

Reading skills are skills that can never truly be mastered. As long as you work on it, you can always improve reading skills. Read the passage that follows and focus on the content. After you have read the passage, answer the questions that follow.

Equal Employment Opportunity Policy

Northwest Product Company (Northwest) is an Equal Opportunity employer. It is the policy of Northwest to give equal opportunity to all qualified individuals without regard to race, color, religion, gender, age, national origin, ancestry, marital status, sexual orientation, the presence of any sensory, mental, or physical disability as outlined in the Americans with Disabilities Act.

All employment practices shall provide that all individuals be recruited, hired, trained, assigned, advanced, compensated, and retained on the basis of their qualifications, job performance, and other business-related criteria only and treated equally in all other respects without regard to their status as a member of any protected class. It shall be the responsibility of every supervisor and management team member to further the implementation of this policy and ensure compliance by subordinates.

Supervisory and management personnel, as well as those responsible for hiring new employees, must take affirmative action in the elimination of any possible discrimination toward employees and applicants for employment with Northwest in all categories and levels of employment and employee relations.

Reading Questions

1. What does it mean for Northwest to be an Equal Opportunity employer?

_____

_____

_____

_____

_____

2. How are individuals who are members of a protected class treated by Northwest?

_____

_____

_____

_____

3. Within the Company, who is responsible for making sure that equal opportunities are available for all?

_____

_____

_____

_____

CHAPTER 10 Marketing

Part 1: Content Review

Matching

Choose the letter of the correct term for each definition.

Terms:

A. marketing
B. promotion
C. product
D. marketing plan

E. marketing mix
F. target market
G. employee engagement
H. relationship selling

I. routine buying decision
J. external influence

1. _____ An emotional connection or commitment of the employee to the employer.

2. _____ The process of communicating with potential customers in an effort to influence their buying behavior.

3. _____ A specific group of customers whose needs a company will focus on satisfying.

4. _____ A document describing business and marketing objectives and the strategies and tactics to achieve them.

5. _____ Consists of dynamic activities that identify, anticipate, and satisfy customer demand while making a profit.

6. _____ The strategy for using the elements of product, price, place, and promotion.

7. _____ A purchase made quickly and with little thought.

8. _____ Motivators or change factors from outside the business.

9. _____ Anything that can be bought or sold.

10. _____ Focuses on building long-term relationships with customers.

Multiple Choice

Choose the letter of the correct answer to each question.

1. _____ Which of the following is an element of the marketing concept?
   A. Customer satisfaction
   B. Vendor satisfaction
   C. Behavioral segmentation
   D. All of the above.

2. _____ The four Ps of marketing include product, price, place, and _____.
   A. prime location
   B. progressive marketing
   C. promotion
   D. production

3. _____ The process of dividing the market into smaller groups is _____.
   A. market planning
   B. market segmentation
   C. promotion
   D. situational influence

4. _____ Dividing the market by certain preferences or lifestyle choices is _____.
   A. demographic segmentation
   B. psychographic segmentation
   C. mass marketing
   D. target marketing

5. _____ A detailed description of the typical consumer in a market segment is a _____.
   A. customer profile
   B. psychological profile
   C. marketing plan
   D. target market

6. _____ Businesses that sell primarily to individual consumers are in the _____ market.
   A. business-to-consumer (B2C)
   B. business-to-business (B2B)
   C. target
   D. mass

7. _____ Which of the following is *not* an influence on consumer buying behavior?
   A. Social
   B. Psychological
   C. Informational
   D. Situational

8. _____ A purchase made with no planning or research is a(n) _____ buying decision.
   A. routine
   B. extensive
   C. expensive
   D. impulse

9. _____ Which of the following business-to-business (B2B) buying decisions involves a great deal of research and thought?
   A. Repeat purchase
   B. Modified purchase
   C. New purchase
   D. Impulse purchase

10. _____ The _____ level of a business-to-business (B2B) buying decision involves little research and thought.
    A. repeat purchase
    B. modified purchase
    C. new purchase
    D. impulse purchase

Completion

Choose the word(s) that best completes each of the following statements.

1. The _____ is an approach to business that focuses on satisfying customers.

_____

2. _____ is the relationship the customer has with a good, service, or company.

_____

3. The plan that helps a business meet its overall goals and objectives is a(n) _____.

_____

4. Segmenting a market based on where customers live is _____.

_____

Name _____

5. Dividing the market of potential customers by their personal statistics is _____.

_____

6. The influences that make each individual consumer unique and affect buying behavior are _____ influences.

_____

7. The power to sway or produce an effect is a(n) _____.

_____

8. The influences that come from the environment and affect buying consumer behavior are _____ influences.

_____

9. In the business-to-consumer (B2C) market, a(n) _____ buying decision involves a great deal of research and planning.

_____

10. In the business-to-business (B2B) market, _____ influences are motivators or change factors that come from within the business itself.

_____

Part 2: Concept Review

Open Response

Respond to each of the following statements or questions. Use complete sentences.

1. What are the four Ps of marketing? Give an example of a product you buy primarily based on price. Give an example of a product you buy primarily based on place.

   _____

   _____

   _____

   _____

   _____

2. What is demographic segmentation? What are five demographic factors you could collect when segmenting the market in this way?

   _____

   _____

   _____

   _____

   _____

   _____

3. What is mass marketing? What is a potential drawback of mass marketing?

   _____

   _____

   _____

   _____

   _____

4. What is database marketing? Identify and explain an example of database marketing.

   _____

   _____

   _____

   _____

   _____

5. What are the four levels of consumer buying decisions? Identify a product you might purchase at each of the four levels.

_____

_____

_____

_____

_____

_____

Part 3: Math Skills

Statistics

Businesses constantly make decisions that involve various types of numerical data, such as prices, sales, order sizes, and various measurements. A math application which involves the collection, analysis, and interpretation of data is called *statistics*. Some of most commonly used statistical measures are the *mean*, *median*, *mode*, and *range*.

The mean is also called the *average*, which is calculated with the following formula:

$$\frac{\text{sum of data entries}}{\text{number of data entries}} = \text{mean}$$

The median is the middle number in the data set after it is organized from smallest to largest. If there are an even number of data entries, add the two middle numbers and divide by 2. For example, if a data range consisted of the numbers 1, 2, 3, 4, 5, the median would be 3. If a data range consisted of the numbers 1, 2, 3, 4, 5, 6, the median would be 3 + 4 divided by 2, which equals 3.5.

The mode is the number in the data set that appears the most. If no number appears more than once, there is no mode.

The range is the difference between the largest and smallest number in the data set and is found using the following formula:

$$\text{largest data entry} - \text{smallest data entry} = \text{range}$$

Answer the following questions involving statistics.

1. Jumpin' Jack is a manufacturer of backyard trampolines. The following are the sales and profit figures for each of the five years from 2011 to 2015.

   2015
   Sales: $417,000
   Profit: $48,600

   2014
   Sales: $355,000
   Profit: $37,900

   2013
   Sales: $339,000
   Profit: $34,000

   2012
   Sales: $312,000
   Profit: $29,600

   2011
   Sales: $298,000
   Profit: $19,800

   A. Calculate the mean sales for Jumpin' Jack's last five years.

   _____

   _____

   B. Calculate the mean profit for Jumpin' Jack's last five years.

   _____

   _____

2. Jumpin' Jack sells five different trampoline models at the following prices:
   $199, $279, $499, $899, and $1,299
   A. Calculate the mean price of the trampolines.

   _____

   _____

B. What is the median price of the trampolines?

_____

_____

C. What is the mode of the trampoline prices?

_____

_____

D. Calculate the range of the trampoline prices.

_____

_____

3. Grand Party Supply operates a chain of party supply stores. The following are the number of piñatas that it has sold over the past seven months.
   - March: 526
   - April: 511
   - May: 599
   - June: 545
   - July: 577
   - August: 489
   - September: 647

What is the average number of piñatas sold over this period?

_____

_____

4. Grand Party Supply has seven stores in Ohio. The size of each store, measured in square feet, is as follows:
   - Store #1: 15,000
   - Store #2: 14,000
   - Store #3: 14,000
   - Store #4: 19,000
   - Store #5: 17,000
   - Store #6: 18,000
   - Store #7: 38,000

A. Calculate the mean store size.

_____

_____

B. Calculate the median store size.

_____

_____

C. Calculate the mode of the store sizes.

_____

_____

D. Calculate the range of store sizes.

_____

_____

5. Refer to the data in the previous problem. Grand Party Supply will open a new 44,000 square foot store next year. Taking the new store into consideration, recalculate the following:

A. Mean store size

_____

_____

B. Median store size

_____

_____

C. Mode of the store sizes

_____

_____

D. Range of store sizes

_____

_____

Part 4: Communication Skills

Writing

Successful employees continuously develop their communication skills. One way to develop communication skills is by working on your vocabulary. *Homonyms* are words that sound alike but have different meanings. Sometimes they are confused and used incorrectly in sentences.

Section I

Choose the correct homonym for each of the sentences.

1. The *affect/effect* of higher gasoline prices is less driving.

   _____

2. Sales of ice cream jumped dramatically during the unusually hot *weather/whether*.

   _____

3. Theft by employees caused the business to *lose/loose* a large amount of inventory.

   _____

4. The business owner needed to raise investment *capitol/capital* to open a factory.

   _____

5. Ace Trucking opened a new terminal in Lansing, the *capitol/capital* of Michigan.

   _____

6. The salesperson did not *hear/here* the customer ask for assistance.

   _____

7. *Who's/Whose* working in the ticket office today?

   _____

8. The customers were dissatisfied and took *their/there* business elsewhere.

   _____

9. I think *your/you're* the best accountant in this firm.

   _____

10. The prices at Victory Electronics were *too/to* high to attract many customers.

    _____

11. A guiding business *principle/principal* at Efficient Furnace is to install and repair furnaces with great care and at fair prices.

    _____

12. *There/Their* is too much clutter in the manager's office.

    _____

Section II

Next, choose a homonym for each of the following words.

13. Wear

_____

14. Made

_____

15. Way

_____

16. Mail

_____

17. Swayed

_____

18. Band

_____

19. Cell

_____

20. Paws

_____

21. Days

_____

22. Plain

_____

23. Reel

_____

24. Break

_____

25. Great

_____

CHAPTER 11   Product, Price, and Place

Part 1: Content Review

Matching

Choose the letter of the correct term for each definition.

Terms:

A. intangible
B. warranty
C. quality
D. guarantee
E. price floor

F. loss leader
G. markup
H. base price
I. e-tailers
J. supply chain

1. _____ Pricing an item much lower than the current market price or the cost of acquiring the product.

2. _____ The general price at which the company expects to sell the product.

3. _____ Something that cannot be touched.

4. _____ The minimum price set by the government for certain goods and services that it thinks are being priced too low.

5. _____ A written document that states the quality of a product with a promise to correct certain problems that might occur.

6. _____ The amount added to the cost to determine the selling price.

7. _____ A promise that a product has a certain quality or will perform in a certain way.

8. _____ Retailers that sell products through websites.

9. _____ The businesses, people, and activities involved in turning raw materials into products and delivering them to end users.

10. _____ An indicator of a product's excellence.

Multiple Choice

Choose the letter of the correct answer to each question.

1. _____ Which of the following is a characteristic of a service?
   A. Can be stored
   B. Can be repeated in exactly the same way
   C. Mass produced
   D. Intangible

2. _____ Which of the following is an example of a basic category of consumer product?
   A. Convenience good
   B. Process material
   C. Component part
   D. Raw materials

3. _____ Which of the following is *not* a business product category in the business-to-business (B2B) market?
   A. Raw materials
   B. Process materials
   C. Major equipment
   D. Shopping goods

4. _____ The price of a good or service must _____.
   A. be lower than what customers are willing to pay
   B. be below any government price floor
   C. cover the cost of producing and selling the product
   D. not be below the manufacturer's suggested retail price (MSRP)

5. _____ Which of the following is an example of a pricing objective?
   A. Minimize cost
   B. Minimize profit
   C. Maximize profit
   D. Minimize the product life cycle

6. _____ During which stage of the product life cycle are the sales and prices of products stable?
   A. Introduction
   B. Growth
   C. Maturity
   D. Decline

7. _____ A product starts making a profit after reaching the _____.
   A. growth stage of the product life cycle
   B. break-even point
   C. price ceiling
   D. mass market

8. _____ The path of selling goods or services directly from a manufacturer to end users without using intermediaries is the _____.
   A. supply chain
   B. direct channel
   C. indirect channel
   D. pipeline

9. _____ Which is *not* a basic type of product created by a producer?
   A. Natural resources
   B. Transportation
   C. Agricultural products
   D. Finished goods

10. _____ Buyers and sellers are brought together by _____.
    A. agents
    B. wholesalers
    C. distributors
    D. rack jobbers

Completion

Choose the word(s) that best completes each of the following statements.

1. The _____ price is the amount a customer pays for a product.

_____

2. The _____ is the stages a product goes through from its beginning to end.

_____

3. A reduced per-item price for larger numbers of an item purchased is a(n) _____.

   _____

4. The practice of _____ is advertising one product with the intent of persuading customers to buy a more expensive item when they arrive in the store.

   _____

5. The practice of setting very low prices to remove competition is _____.

   _____

6. Raising prices on certain kinds of goods to an excessively high level during an emergency is _____.

   _____

7. The physical movement of products through the channel of distribution is _____.

   _____

8. Companies that organize shipments are _____.

   _____

9. A(n) _____ purchases large amounts of goods directly from manufacturers, stores them, and then resells in smaller quantities to various retailers.

   _____

10. The process of separating a large quantity of goods into smaller quantities is _____.

   _____

Part 2: Concept Review

Open Response

Respond to each of the following statements or questions. Use complete sentences.

1. What is the difference between the list price of a product and the selling price?

_____

_____

_____

_____

_____

_____

2. What are the four stages of the product life cycle? Explain changes in the price of a product throughout its life cycle.

_____

_____

_____

_____

_____

_____

_____

_____

3. What are five common discount pricing techniques used in the business-to-business (B2B) market? Briefly describe each.

_____

_____

_____

_____

_____

_____

_____

_____

_____

4. What is an indirect channel of distribution? Who are the people and businesses that may be involved in indirect channels?

_____

_____

_____

_____

_____

5. What are the six main methods of transportation? Choose an item you purchase regularly and identify the methods of transportation used to get the product from the manufacturer to you.

_____

_____

_____

_____

_____

_____

Part 3: Math Skills

Multistep Mathematics

Businesses must set appropriate prices for their products to make a profit. However, companies do not set prices at random. There are a number of important policies and strategies involved, some of which involve multistep mathematics.

Answer the following questions about pricing.

1. A unit price is based on a standard unit of measurement, such as an ounce or inch. It is used to compare the prices of different sized items. The formula for calculating unit price is:

$$\frac{price}{number\ of\ units} = unit\ price$$

Tropical Sun Coconut Water is sold at several retailers. Calculate the unit price of each container and determine which retailer offers the best value.

A. Better Health Store

   Price: $2.79

   Size: 12 ounce can

   _____

   _____

B. Fresh 'N More Market

   Price: $4.99

   Size: 20 ounce can

   _____

   _____

C. Mega Warehouse Club

   Price: $39.99

   Size: 24 pack case of 12 ounce cans

   _____

   _____

2. A break-even point is when revenue from sales equals costs. It is calculated using the following formula:

$$\frac{fixed\ costs}{selling\ price - variable\ costs} = break\text{-}even\ point$$

Jogging Boy Company manufactures a unique jogging stroller that has a lightweight frame and holds up to three children. The stroller sells for $399. The variable cost to manufacture each stroller is $165. The company's annual fixed costs are $135,000. How many strollers does Jogging Boy need to sell to break even for the year?

   _____

   _____

3. Cost-based pricing sets a base price by adding a markup to the product cost. It is calculated using the following formula:

$$cost + markup = base\ price$$

Kale Power makes a delicious snack bar that is very high in beta carotene and vitamin K. The cost to make a 3 ounce bar is $0.55. Kale Power marks up the item by $0.95 to help cover fixed costs and contribute an acceptable profit to the business. What is the base price?

   _____

   _____

4. Another method of calculating a base price is to add a *percentage* markup to the product cost. Percentage markup is calculated using the following formula:

$$cost + (cost \times markup\ percentage) = price$$

Applying the same markup percentage to items can help achieve a more consistent level of profits. Banana Dragon manufactures high-quality water shirts for surfing, water skiing, and other water sports. The company adds a 90 percent markup to its product cost when setting the base price for its various styles. The following shows the product cost for three different shirt styles. Calculate the markup and base price for each style.

A. Big

Product Cost: $23

_____

_____

B. High Tide

Product Cost: $22

_____

_____

C. Dragon Lagoon

Product Cost: $27

_____

_____

5. Banana Dragon's High Tide water shirt style has been extremely popular, while the Dragon Lagoon style has not. The company decides to raise its markup on High Tide style to 125 percent and reduce the markup on Dragon Lagoon to 75 percent. What is the new markup and base price for each style?

A. High Tide

Product Cost: $22

_____

_____

B. Dragon Lagoon

Product Cost: $27

_____

_____

Part 4: Communication Skills

Listening

Listening skills are essential when working in any retail position. Try to improve your listening skills by analyzing one of your instructor's classroom presentations. More specifically, identify how your instructor conveys information to you and the other students by answering the following questions.

1. What was the topic or main point?

_____

_____

_____

2. Did you clearly understand the message? If not, why?

_____

_____

_____

3. Were there any nonverbal messages transmitted? If so, what were they?

_____

_____

_____

4. Did you or other students give feedback to your instructor? If so, what was some of the feedback?

_____

_____

_____

Share your analysis with your instructor to see if you understood the main points of the lesson. Then answer the following questions:

5. Who is responsible for your understanding of the lesson—you or your instructor?

_____

_____

6. Who is the better judge of how well you understood the message—you or your instructor?

_____

_____

Discuss your analysis and the feedback with your class. Did most of your classmates agree on the message that was transmitted? Summarize your analysis in the space provided.

_____

_____

_____

_____

_____

CHAPTER 12 / Promotion

Part 1: Content Review

Matching
Choose the letter of the correct term for each definition.

Terms:

A. promotion
B. persuasion
C. sender
D. decoding
E. feedback

F. advertising
G. direct marketing
H. tagline
I. typeface
J. layout

1. _____ Uses logic to change a belief or get people to take a certain action.
2. _____ Type of advertising sent directly to individual customers without the use of a third party.
3. _____ The person who has a message to communicate.
4. _____ A phrase or sentence that summarizes an essential part of the product or business.
5. _____ The receiver's response to the sender and concludes the communication process.
6. _____ The arrangement of the headline, copy, and art on a page.
7. _____ The process of communicating with potential customers in an effort to influence their buying behavior.
8. _____ A particular style for the printed letters of the alphabet, punctuation, and numbers.
9. _____ Any nonpersonal communication paid for by an identified sponsor.
10. _____ The translation of a message into terms the receiver can understand.

Multiple Choice
Choose the letter of the correct answer to each question.

1. _____ In the communication process, _____ is how the message is translated.
   A. hearing
   B. translating
   C. feedback
   D. decoding

2. _____ One of the common elements in a promotional mix is _____.
   A. place
   B. pricing
   C. personal selling
   D. marketing

3. _____ Coupons, rebates, and loyalty programs are part of _____.
   A. sales promotion
   B. advertising
   C. public relations
   D. personal selling

4. _____ Attention, interest, desire, and action (AIDA) are elements of a _____.
   A. tagline
   B. promotional campaign
   C. press release
   D. point of purchase display (POP)

5. _____ Any direct contact between a salesperson and a customer is _____.
   A. public relations
   B. public communication
   C. personal selling
   D. personal promotion

6. _____ A coordinated series of link ads with a single idea or theme is a(n) _____.
   A. hook
   B. brand name
   C. advertising campaign
   D. tagline

7. _____ Which is *not* a step in the process of creating an advertising campaign?
   A. Set campaign goals
   B. Encode the message
   C. Create the message
   D. Establish the metrics

8. _____ The elements of an advertisement include headline, copy, graphics, and _____.
   A. marquee
   B. persuasion
   C. metrics
   D. signature

9. _____ The _____ is the name given to a product consisting of words, letters, or numbers that can be spoken.
   A. brand name
   B. logo
   C. tagline
   D. hook

10. _____ The main governmental agency that monitors the actions of advertisers is the _____.
    A. Federal Standards Commission (FSC)
    B. Federal Bureau of Investigation (FBI)
    C. Federal Trade Commission (FTC)
    D. Securities and Exchange Commission (SEC)

Completion

Choose the word(s) that best completes each of the following statements.

1. _____ promotion focuses on promoting the company rather than the product.

   _____

2. The _____ process is a series of actions on the part of the sender and the receiver of a message and the path the message follows.

   _____

3. A combination of elements used in a promotional campaign is the _____.

   _____

4. An overhanging structure containing a sign at the entrance of the store is a(n) _____.

   _____

5. Communication skills that promote goodwill between a business and the public is _____.

_____

6. A promotion strategy that uses multiple elements to communicate and interact with customers is _____ marketing.

_____

7. A(n) _____ outlines the goals, primary message, budget, and target market for different ad campaigns.

_____

8. A picture, design, or graphic image that represents the brand is a(n) _____.

_____

9. _____ is the use of electronic media to promote a product or brand.

_____

10. The _____ identifies the person or company paying for an ad.

_____

Part 2: Concept Review

Open Response

Respond to each of the following statements or questions. Use complete sentences.

1. What are the six elements of the communication process? Explain the activity in each step of the process.

_____

_____

_____

_____

_____

_____

_____

2. Explain the concept of integrated marketing communications.

_____

_____

_____

_____

_____

_____

3. How do marketers determine if an advertising campaign is successful?

_____

_____

_____

_____

_____

Name _____

4. Advertising benefits business, but it can also benefit society. Identify three ways advertising can benefit society.

_____

_____

_____

_____

_____

_____

_____

5. Promotion has definite goals. It is used to inform, persuade, or remind the audience of a message. Give examples of messages that a professional football team might send its audience that inform, persuade, or remind.

_____

_____

_____

_____

_____

_____

_____

Part 3: Math Skills

Mixed Mathematics

It is essential to understand and be able to perform basic mathematical tasks in order to handle many business functions. This is especially true in retailing, where some of the most important tasks include correctly and efficiently ringing up sales, accurately handling and distributing change in cash transactions, and calculating refunds and adjustments.

Answer the following questions involving sales transactions.

1. Cash, debit card, and credit card transactions must include a sales tax in many states. The formulas for calculating sales tax and total sale amount are as follows:

    sales total × sales tax rate = sales tax

    sales total + sales tax = total sale amount

    The sales tax is added to the sales total to equal the total sale amount, which is collected from the customer.

    You own an appliance store in a state with 6 percent sales tax. A customer purchases a convection oven priced at $1,199. How much is the sales tax? How much is the total sale amount that you collect from the customer?

    _____

    _____

    _____

2. Master Auto Service is an auto repair shop in a state that charges 5 percent sales tax on merchandise, but no tax on services. The following is a service order for a recent customer:

    New Headlamp: $124.99

    Halogen Bulb: $36.99

    Installation: $79

    Total: $240.98

    Calculate the sales tax on this order and the total sale amount that the customer must pay.

    _____

    _____

    _____

3. The Wild and Wacky Water Park charges $24 for adult admission and $12.50 for children under the age of 12. A customer requests two adult tickets and one child's ticket and gives the cashier four $20 bills. The cashier gives the customer $18 in change.

    A. Is this the correct amount of change? If not, calculate the correct amount.

    _____

    _____

    _____

    B. The cash drawer at the water park has the following denominations of bills and coins. Indicate how many coins and bills the cashier should give the customer.

    $20: _____

    $10: _____

    $5: _____

    $1: _____

    $0.25: _____

    $0.10: _____

    $0.05: _____

    $0.01: _____

4. Sentinel Locksmith operates in a state with 4.5 percent sales tax. A customer recently made the following purchase:

Item: Dead Bolt Lock	$99.95
Item: Window Locks	$49.95
Item: Door Knob Set	$29.99
Total:	$179.89
Sales Tax:	$8.10
Total Sale:	$187.99

The customer now wants to return the window locks set for a refund. Calculate the refund amount.

_____

_____

_____

5. A customer at Diplomat Tuxedo is picking up a rented tuxedo and accessories for a school event. However, the sales associate learns there was a problem in altering the tuxedo, and it will not be available until tomorrow. The sales associate apologizes and offers to reduce the bill by 25 percent because of the inconvenience. The original bill was $139.00.

A. What is the dollar amount of the 25 percent reduction? What is the bill after the reduction?

_____

_____

B. What is the final bill with 4.5 percent sales tax?

_____

_____

Part 4: Communication Skills

Reading

In business, procedures are generally set up as a series of steps or directions. It is important to be able to read, understand, and abide by these directions. Read the passage below and focus on the content. After you have read the passage, answer the questions that follow.

How to Direct to Ensure Understanding of Trainee

Step 1. Preparing a Trainee
- Put the trainee at ease.
- Get the trainee excited about the new job.

Step 2. Present the Job
- Tell, show, and illustrate the job carefully and patiently.
- Stress the key points—explain the reasons why they are important.
- Instruct and demonstrate clearly and visibly—one step at a time and in small amounts with no more than can be understood.
- Ask questions to uncover understandings and misunderstandings.
- Repeat instructions if deemed necessary through the questioning that took place.

Step 3. Have Trainee Perform the Task
- Have the trainee walk through the task while the instructor observes closely and corrects errors.
- Have the trainee complete the job a second time while explaining the key procedures to the trainer.
- Ask the trainee what, why, when, and who questions during and following the demonstration.
- Have the trainee continue doing the job as the trainer observes the performance until the performance is satisfactory.

Step 4. Follow Up
- Allow the trainee to work independently.
- Designate to whom the trainee should go for help if needed.
- Check the trainee frequently and watch follow through on key components of the task.
- Encourage questions by not rushing the trainee.
- Slowly taper off coaching and conclude follow-ups.

Reading Questions

1. There are four major steps presented in this passage. Do you think they need to be followed in order or can they be followed randomly?

   _____

   _____

   _____

2. If you were the person working with a trainee, would you consider these directions complete? Are there any directions which you consider unnecessary or confusing? Briefly explain.

   _____

   _____

   _____

   _____

   _____

   _____

CHAPTER 13 / Selling

Part 1: Content Review

Matching

Choose the letter of the correct term for each definition.

Terms:

A. personal selling

B. preapproach

C. cold calling

D. close

E. buying signals

F. substitute selling

G. customer service

H. transaction

I. online support

J. customer support team

1. _____ Making contact with people who are not expecting a sales contact.

2. _____ The technique of showing products that are different from the originally requested product.

3. _____ The way in which a business provides services before, during, and after a purchase.

4. _____ Direct contact with a prospective customer with the objective of selling a product.

5. _____ Information and resources available through the Internet.

6. _____ The exchange of payment and product.

7. _____ Employees who assist customers, take orders, and answer questions that come into the company via phone or website.

8. _____ Tasks that are performed before contact is made with a customer.

9. _____ The moment when a customer agrees to buy a product.

10. _____ Verbal or nonverbal signs that a customer is ready to purchase.

Multiple Choice

Choose the letter of the correct answer to each question.

1. _____ Business-to-business selling (B2B) may also be called _____.
   A. field sales
   B. industrial sales
   C. organizational sales
   D. All of the above.

2. _____ An office that is set up for the purpose of receiving and making customer calls is a _____ center.
   A. lead
   B. call
   C. cold call
   D. business-to-customer (B2C)

3. _____ Which of the following approaches is often used in a business-to-consumer (B2C) sales setting?
A. Service
B. Cold call
C. Emotional
D. All of the above.

4. _____ In business-to-consumer (B2C) selling situations, which of the following is a *not* a motive for customers to buy a product?
A. Rational
B. Emotional
C. Transactional
D. Loyalty buying

5. _____ There are three ways to determine customer needs and wants. Which involves body language?
A. Observation
B. Verifying
C. Questioning
D. Listening

6. _____ When a customer raises an objection during a product presentation, the first thing a salesperson should do is _____.
A. agree with the customer
B. pause
C. offer a substitute product
D. end the presentation

7. _____ Overselling is _____.
A. selling more than the customer really wants
B. exceeding the company's sales projection
C. promising more than can be delivered
D. selling after normal business hours

8. _____ Service that meets customer needs, as well as the standards for customer service set by the company, is _____.
A. overselling
B. quality customer service
C. excessive customer service
D. exceptional customer service

9. _____ The customer service mindset is the attitude that the customer _____.
A. needs overselling
B. should spend money
C. needs to listen
D. comes first

10. _____ Which of the following is a common type of online support?
A. Emotional buying
B. E-mail support
C. Cold calling
D. All of the above.

Completion

Choose the word(s) that best completes each of the following statements.

1. In business-to-business (B2B) sales, a(n) _____ salesperson visits with customers at their places of business.

_____

2. Showing the major selling features of a product and how it benefits the customer is _____ selling.

_____

3. The _____ is when the salesperson makes the first in-person contact with a potential customer.

_____

4. Personal reasons *not* to buy are _____.

_____

5. _____ buying motives are based more on feelings than reason.

_____

6. The phrase "going above and beyond" is often used to refer to _____ customer service.

_____

7. Information and resources available to customers through the Internet is _____.

_____

8. A(n) _____ contains answers to customer questions as posted by other customers or product users.

_____

9. After a transaction is complete, it is important for a salesperson to _____ with the customer to ensure the customer is satisfied.

_____

10. Hearing is a physical process, while _____ is an intellectual process.

_____

Part 2: Concept Review

Open Response

Respond to each of the following statements or questions. Use complete sentences.

1. One of the tasks that must be completed before making contact with the customer is to generate leads. What are leads and what are some ways to generate them?

_____

_____

_____

_____

_____

2. What are the six steps in the sales process? Explain the importance of the last step.

_____

_____

_____

_____

_____

_____

_____

_____

3. What are buying signals? Identify some buying signals a salesperson should look for.

_____

_____

_____

_____

_____

4. Explain how websites help a business provide customer support.

_____

_____

_____

_____

_____

5. Determining the customer's needs is the second step is the sales process. Explain how a salesperson can determine the needs of a customer.

_____

_____

_____

_____

_____

_____

_____

_____

Part 3: Math Skills

Percentages

Businesses often calculate percentages as part of their daily activities. A percentage (%) means a part of 100 and is the same as a fraction or decimal. For example, 15 percent is the same as $15 \div 100$ or .15. To calculate the percentage of a number, change the percentage to a decimal and multiply by the number. For example:

Calculate 25 percent of 200.

$$25 \text{ percent of } 200 = \frac{25}{100} \times 200$$

$$.25 \times 200 = 50$$

To determine what percentage one number is of another, divide the first number by the second. Then, convert the quotient into a percentage by moving the decimal two places to the right. For example:

What percentage is 50 of 200?

$$\frac{50}{200} = .25 \rightarrow 25\%$$

Answer the following questions involving percentages.

1. Supply Plus Office Warehouse is offering a 20 percent discount on all ink cartridges. Calculate the discount amount on the following cartridges, rounding to the nearest cent:

   A. #22 Black
      Price: $13.99

      _____

      _____

   B. #22 Color
      Price: $19.99

      _____

      _____

   C. #22 Twin Pack
      Price: $29.99

      _____

   D. #22 XL Black
      Price: $31.49

      _____

      _____

   E. #22 XL Color
      Price: $48.49

      _____

      _____

2. Linear Computers is offering refurbished computers at a special clearance price. Calculate the price reduction for each of the following computers. Then, calculate the price reduction as a percentage of the original price.

A. Linear 15 inch Laptop
Original Price: $599
Clearance Price: $499

_____

_____

B. Linear 8 inch Tablet
Original Price: $199
Clearance Price: $149

_____

_____

C. Linear 17 inch Laptop
Original Price: $799
Clearance Price: $549

_____

_____

D. Linear Pro 23 inch All-in-One
Original Price: $1,099
Clearance Price: $879

_____

_____

3. Sales for X-Pert Pest Control were $365,000 last year. This year, the owner is expecting sales to be 8 percent higher. How much is this sales increase?

_____

_____

4. Pro Tour Mills makes golf shirts. Last year the company sold 490,000 golf shirts. Of this total, 119,000 shirts were cotton and 371,000 were lightweight polyester. What percent of shirts were lightweight polyester?

_____

_____

5. Refer to the previous problem. Pro Tour Mills expects to sell 15 percent more golf shirts this year than last year. However, the owner thinks cotton shirts will not be as popular, and that this style will comprise only 15 percent of its total sales. Calculate the number of golf shirts Pro Tour expects to sell this year. Then, calculate the number it expects to sell in both cotton and lightweight polyester.

_____

_____

_____

_____

Part 4: Communication Skills

Nonverbal Communication

Not all communication is verbal. When working with the public, it is important to understand nonverbal communication. An excellent way to learn about nonverbal communication is to observe your instructor during the presentation of a lesson. In the space provided, identify ten gestures, facial expressions, and other types of body language you observe. Describe the meaning that each communicates.

1. _____
   _____
   _____
   _____

2. _____
   _____
   _____
   _____

3. _____
   _____
   _____
   _____

4. _____
   _____
   _____
   _____

5. _____
   _____
   _____
   _____

6. _____
   _____
   _____
   _____

7. _____
   _____
   _____
   _____

Name _____

8. _____

_____

_____

_____

9. _____

_____

_____

_____

10. _____

_____

_____

_____

Notes

CHAPTER 14 / Risk Management

Part 1: Content Review

Matching

Choose the letter of the correct term for each definition.

Terms:

A. cyber insurance
B. natural risk
C. market risk
D. risk management
E. insurance

F. premium
G. claim
H. deductible
I. property insurance
J. disability insurance

1. _____ Covers loss incurred from cyberattacks, such as data breaches and computer viruses.

2. _____ A financial service used to protect against loss.

3. _____ The process of documenting a loss against an insurance policy.

4. _____ Provides some financial income to employees who become sick or injured due to a nonwork related event or condition.

5. _____ The amount the insured is responsible for paying when a claim is made.

6. _____ The potential that the target market for new goods or services is much less than originally projected.

7. _____ The amount the insured pays for insurance coverage.

8. _____ Covers losses and damage to the assets of a business caused by a variety of events, such as floods, fire, smoke, and vandalism.

9. _____ A situation caused by an act of nature.

10. _____ The process of evaluating risk and finding ways to minimize or manage loss.

Multiple Choice

Choose the letter of the correct answer to each question.

1. _____ Which of the following is *not* one of the four basic types of risk?
   A. Natural
   B. Economic
   C. Market
   D. Controllable

2. _____ _____ risks are situations that cannot be avoided, but can be minimized by purchasing insurance or creating a risk management plan.
   A. Economic
   B. Controllable
   C. Uncontrollable
   D. Market

3. _____ _____ risks are situations that cannot be predicted or covered by purchasing insurance.
   A. Economic
   B. Controllable
   C. Uncontrollable
   D. Market

4. _____ Which of the following is one of the basic ways to manage risk?
   A. Avoidance
   B. Assumption
   C. Adherence
   D. Reliance

5. _____ A _____ risk is a risk with a possibility of loss, but no possibility of gain.
   A. controllable
   B. pure
   C. speculative
   D. natural

6. _____ A(n) _____ provides the insured with protection against economic loss for a fee.
   A. broker
   B. independent agent
   C. policyholder
   D. insurer

7. _____ _____ liability insurance protects against losses that result from legal issues.
   A. General
   B. Product
   C. Professional
   D. Controllable

8. _____ Which of the following is *not* an example of commercial insurance?
   A. Commercial property
   B. Commercial auto
   C. Commercial professional
   D. Equipment breakdown

9. _____ Employees who are injured at work are covered by _____ insurance.
   A. disability
   B. unemployment
   C. business interruption
   D. workers' compensation

10. _____ A(n) _____ defines the type of losses that are covered, amount of coverage in dollars, and other conditions to which the insured and insurer agree.
    A. insurance claim
    B. insurance policy
    C. commission agreement
    D. fidelity bond

Completion

Choose the word(s) that best completes each of the following statements.

1. A situation that occurs when business activities suffer due to changes in the US or world economy is a(n) _____ risk.

_____

2. A negative situation caused by actions of people is a(n) _____ risk.

_____

3. A risk that can result in either financial gain or financial loss is a(n) _____ risk.

_____

4. A(n) _____ risk is one that an insurance company will not cover.

_____

5. _____ is a risk management strategy in which a business takes steps to eliminate risk.

_____

6. A(n) _____ agent is an insurance agent who works for multiple insurance companies.

_____

7. A(n) _____ agent works for only one insurance company.

_____

8. _____ insurance covers financial losses caused by the actions or negligence of a person or business.

_____

9. A loss caused by employee actions, such as theft or embezzlement, is covered by a(n) _____.

_____

10. _____ insurance provides certain benefits to workers who have lost their jobs through no fault of their own.

_____

Part 2: Concept Review

Open Response

Respond to each of the following statements or questions. Use complete sentences.

1. What are four basic risk management strategies? Briefly describe each strategy.

   _____

   _____

   _____

   _____

   _____

   _____

   _____

2. An orthodontist starts a new practice and purchases insurance to cover the office and equipment in the event of fire, theft, or certain natural disasters. Is any other insurance needed before seeing patients? Explain your answer.

   _____

   _____

   _____

   _____

   _____

3. Identify three ways employees can pose a risk to their employers. How can these risks be managed?

   _____

   _____

   _____

   _____

   _____

   _____

   _____

4. Insurance companies offer many different types of liability insurance for businesses. What is data breach insurance? What is covered?

_____

_____

_____

_____

_____

5. Identify a business you might be interested in starting. Make a list of ten different business activities that would pose a risk to your business that could result in a loss. Classify each activity as either a controllable or uncontrollable risk. For each risk, indicate if you think it can be avoided, reduced, transferred, or must be assumed.

_____

_____

_____

_____

_____

_____

_____

_____

_____

_____

_____

Part 3: Math Skills

Basic Math

Businesses assume risk every day involving many factors, including fire, storms, vandalism, and theft. They try to reduce risks with proper planning and insurance coverage. This requires basic math skills.

Answer the following questions involving risk planning.

1. Computer Tech Solutions provides software support and computer repairs in a leased building. The owner pays $117 a month for a business insurance policy that covers business equipment, store fixtures, and liability. What is the annual cost of this insurance coverage?

   _____

   _____

2. The Grand Inn is a small hotel that the owner purchased 31 years ago. The owner wants insurance to replace the hotel and furnishings in the event it is destroyed by fire or storm. The estimated cost of reconstruction is $1,950,000. New furniture and hotel supplies would cost $175,000. It would cost an additional $20,000 to meet new city ordinances that were enacted since the hotel was built. How much insurance coverage does the owner need?

   _____

   _____

3. Maggie Johnson Specialties is an antiques and collectibles dealer. Johnson has insurance to cover the cost of inventory, which was purchased for $335,000. However, some of the antiques and collectibles in inventory have risen in value since they were purchased. The owner estimates that it would cost $500,000 to replace the store's inventory today. How much is the owner currently at risk if all of the store's inventory were lost or stolen?

   _____

   _____

4. Simpson's Garden Center has insurance that covers 90 percent of the damage to its store and greenhouse from fire, storm, and vandalism. A windstorm causes $28,000 damage to its greenhouse. How much is covered by insurance? How much will be paid by the owner?

   _____

   _____

5. Speed Wheels has insurance on its race car track that covers up to $150,000 in damage, with a $7,500 deductible. This means that Speed Wheels must pay the first $7,500 before the insurance coverage begins. The race track is vandalized and incurs $14,200 in damages. How much will the insurance pay toward this damage?

   _____

   _____

Part 4: Communication Skills

Reading

When reading company policies, it is important to seek explanation if you do not understand something. Failure to do so may result in miscommunication between you and your superiors. Read the passage that follows and focus on the content. After you have read the passage, respond to the questions that follow.

Commitment to Safety

Safety is a part of every employee's job responsibility. It is a major part of YOUR responsibility here at Elroy Company. Every employee should perform every job in a safe manner. Correct and safe procedures, tools, equipment, and protective devices should be used at all times. If you have any questions about these, please talk to your supervisor or the Human Resources Director. You must immediately report any possible safety hazard, near-miss incidents, or injury to your supervisor, the Human Resources Director, or other member of the management team. If you suffer an occupational injury or illness, no matter how minor, YOU MUST REPORT IT IMMEDIATELY to your supervisor or the Human Resources Director. Failure to report occupational injuries and illnesses, accidents, or near-miss incidents as they occur is grounds for disciplinary action, up to and including termination.

This section of the *Employee Handbook* is intended to provide guidelines on how the Company can and will fulfill our responsibilities for the protection of our employees and premises. It is not intended to be a substitute for common sense and an employee's own diligence. Nor is it expected to replace sound safety policies and procedures, which are carefully monitored, enforced, reviewed, and corrected to establish the high standards for safety we strive to achieve. This section cannot possibly address every safety situation; however, it does endeavor toward continuous improvement and compliance with all applicable state, local, and federal safety laws and regulations.

We ask that you recognize safety hazards and remain alert while performing your duties here. It is only through a combined effort from you and Elroy Company that we will all remain safe, secure, and healthy.

Our safety belief is simple: "Continuous improvement of our Safety Program through training, awareness, motivation, and self-evaluation are keys to achieving and maintaining an accident-free workplace."

Reading Questions

1. Is Elroy Company solely responsible for employee safety?

_____

_____

_____

_____

2. If a safety hazard is found, to whom and when should it be reported?

_____

_____

_____

_____

3. What purpose does the Employee Handbook serve in employee safety? Does it address every possible safety situation?

_____

_____

_____

_____

_____

CHAPTER 15 Money and Banking

Part 1: Content Review

Matching
Choose the letter of the correct term for each definition.

Terms:

A. money
B. security
C. credit card
D. financial exchange
E. electronic funds transfer (EFT)

F. depository institution
G. deposit
H. finance company
I. checking account
J. savings account

1. _____ A bank account used by depositors to accumulate money for future use.

2. _____ A financial institution that makes money by issuing loans.

3. _____ The process of transferring money from one individual or organization to another.

4. _____ Anything of value that is accepted in return for goods and services.

5. _____ A type of financial investment issued by a corporation, government, or other organization.

6. _____ A financial institution that accepts money from a customer and deposits it into the customer's account.

7. _____ A plastic card that the holder uses to make credit purchases up to an authorized amount.

8. _____ Money placed into an account.

9. _____ Movement of money over an online network from one financial institution to another.

10. _____ A bank account that allows the owner to make deposits, write checks, and withdraw money.

Multiple Choice
Choose the letter of the correct answer to each question.

1. _____ Money serves which of the following functions?
   A. Medium of exchange
   B. Unit of value
   C. Store of value
   D. All of the above.

2. _____ To be useful and meaningful in an economy, money must be _____.
   A. plentiful
   B. reproducible
   C. divisible
   D. renewable

3. _____ The _____ is our nation's central bank.
   A. United States Mint
   B. Federal Reserve System
   C. United States Treasury
   D. US Bureau of Engraving and Printing

4. _____ Action taken to manage the supply of money and interest rates in an economy is _____.
   A. monetary policy
   B. fiscal policy
   C. financial intermediation
   D. financial control

5. _____ A bank-issued _____ allows customers to pay for purchases directly from their checking account.
   A. banknote
   B. credit card
   C. debit card
   D. letter of credit

6. _____ The largest category of depository institutions is _____.
   A. commercial banks
   B. investment banks
   C. credit unions
   D. savings and loan institutions

7. _____ An insurance company is an example of a _____.
   A. depository institution
   B. nondepository institution
   C. finance company
   D. thrift institution

8. _____ General banking services do *not* include _____.
   A. checking accounts
   B. savings accounts
   C. letters of credit
   D. electronic banking

9. _____ A(n) _____ is a prearranged amount of credit that is available for a business to use as needed.
   A. letter of credit
   B. line of credit
   C. electronic funds transfer (EFT)
   D. savings account

10. _____ An independent government agency that provides deposit insurance in the event of a bank failure is the
    _____.
    A. Federal Reserve System (the Fed)
    B. Office of Thrift Supervision
    C. Comptroller of the Currency
    D. Federal Deposit Insurance Corporation (FDIC)

Completion

Choose the word(s) that best completes each of the following statements.

1. To _____ is to exchange one good or service for another good or service.

   _____

2. In the United States, the _____ is the official currency of financial exchange.

   _____

3. _____ means that money is a common measure of the worth or price of a good or service.

   _____

4. The mechanism a nation uses to provide and manage money for itself is a(n) _____.

   _____

5. Banks that are part of the Federal Reserve System are known as _____.

_____

6. A nonprofit financial institution that is privately owned and provides banking services for its members is a(n) _____.

_____

7. A financial institution that is involved in trading securities in financial markets is a(n) _____.

_____

8. A(n) _____ is a financial institution that helps businesses raise money for expansion or maintenance of the business.

_____

9. A(n) _____ is a document that guarantees that a buyer will pay the seller the agreed-upon amount and within the time specified.

_____

10. The _____ Act requires clear disclosure of finance charges and annual percentage rates on loans.

_____

Part 2: Concept Review

Open Response

Respond to each of the following statements or questions. Use complete sentences.

1. Identify four basic types of financial exchange. Briefly explain the benefits of each.

_____

_____

_____

_____

_____

_____

_____

_____

2. Explain the role and responsibilities of the Federal Reserve System in the United States.

_____

_____

_____

_____

_____

_____

_____

_____

3. Identify three banking needs that are unique to businesses.

_____

_____

_____

_____

_____

_____

4. Explain the roles of the Federal Deposit Insurance Corporation (FDIC) and National Credit Union Administration (NCUA) in our nation's banking system.

_____

_____

_____

_____

_____

5. What are nondepository institutions? List the four major types of nondepository institutions. Are any of these financial institutions familiar to you? Explain why.

_____

_____

_____

_____

_____

_____

_____

Part 3: Math Skills

Mixed Mathematics

Business owners and employees need to understand how compensation is paid for different jobs and how the compensation is calculated. Compensation can be paid in different ways: hourly wages, salaried employment, and commission. Basic math is essential in understanding each.

Answer the following questions about compensation.

1. One of the most common ways to be paid is by the hour, especially for entry-level employees. Hourly wages are calculated using the following formula:

   hourly wage × number of hours worked = total earnings

   A lifeguard at a water park worked 32 hours last week at an hourly wage of $11.75. Calculate this employee's earnings.

   _____

   _____

2. Federal law requires that employees receive overtime pay for hours worked in excess of 40 hours in a workweek. Overtime pay is at least 1.5 times the regular hourly wage. Using 1.5 as an overtime multiplier, calculate the earnings of a customer service representative who earns $13 an hour and works 48 hours in a week.

   _____

   _____

   _____

3. It is common to pay professionals and managerial staff a salary. A salary is a fixed payment for work, usually paid monthly or twice a month. The formula for calculating the amount of wages received per paycheck is:

$$\frac{\text{annual pay}}{\text{number of pay periods per year}} = \text{amount per paycheck}$$

   An information technology professional earns an annual salary of $66,000 and receives paychecks twice a month. How much is each paycheck?

   _____

   _____

   _____

4. Sometimes a salaried employee can receive a bonus in addition to a regular salary. Bonus amounts may be a fixed amount or be a percentage of an annual salary. For example, a restaurant manager earns a $72,000 annual salary. In addition, once the restaurant achieves a certain profit, the manager receives a 25 percent bonus. Calculate the manager's annual earnings.

   _____

   _____

5. Employees with sales positions often earn a commission. Commission is an added amount that is usually a percentage of a sales transaction and is calculated with the following formula:

   item price × number of items × commission rate = commission

   A salesperson at a flooring store earns $200 a week plus the following commission: 5 percent of hard flooring sales and 4 percent of carpet sales. Calculate earnings for last week if the salesperson sold $11,000 of hard flooring and $12,000 of carpet.

   _____

   _____

   _____

Name _____

Part 4: Communication Skills

Writing

Written forms of communication are necessary when performing the duties of most jobs. Writing for professional communication requires precise word choice and presentation. One of the common rules to follow is to avoid dividing, or hyphenating, words at the end of sentences. This reduces the readability of the written words. However, there are times when this cannot be avoided. When it is necessary to divide a word at the end of a sentence, follow these basic guidelines:

- Do not divide single-syllable words or contractions.
- Divide words between syllables.
- When a word contains a hyphen, divide it at the existing hyphen.
- Divide compound words between the two base words.
- Do not divide proper names.

Follow the guidelines for dividing words to hyphenate the words below.

1. completeness

_____

2. surround

_____

3. instead

_____

4. frequency

_____

5. prepared

_____

6. exclude

_____

7. communication

_____

8. correspondent

_____

9. previous

_____

10. can't

_____

11. textbook

_____

12. graduate

_____

13. sincerely

_____

14. automatically

_____

15. brother-in-law

_____

CHAPTER 16 / Credit

Part 1: Content Review

Matching

Choose the letter of the correct term for each definition.

Terms:

A. credit
B. creditor
C. principal
D. finance charge
E. unsecured credit

F. credit policy
G. credit report
H. credit score
I. credit risk
J. collection agency

1. _____ A company that collects past-due bills for a fee.

2. _____ The total amount paid by a borrower to a lender for the use of credit.

3. _____ The amount of money borrowed.

4. _____ A numerical measure of a loan applicant's creditworthiness at a particular point in time.

5. _____ A record of credit history and financial behavior for a business or individual.

6. _____ An agreement between two parties in which one party lends money or provides goods or services to another party with the understanding that payment will be made at a later date.

7. _____ The party extending credit.

8. _____ Credit granted based on a signed credit agreement.

9. _____ A written set of guidelines used by an organization to determine how many and which customers will be approved for credit.

10. _____ The potential of credit not being repaid.

Multiple Choice

Choose the letter of the correct answer to each question.

1. _____ The party receiving credit is known as the _____.
   A. creditor
   B. debtor
   C. principal
   D. credit agency

2. _____ One of the benefits of credit is _____.
   A. the opportunity to buy costly items
   B. interest charges
   C. finance charges
   D. credit risk

3. _____ Credit loans that require collateral are knows as _____.
   A. secured credit
   B. unsecured credit
   C. open-end credit
   D. installment loans

4. _____ The finance charge for the use of credit has two parts: _____.
   A. interest and credit
   B. interest and principal
   C. interest and fees
   D. fees and APR

5. _____ The total amount paid for the use of credit is based on which of the following factors?
   A. Interest rate charged
   B. Amount of credit used
   C. Length of repayment period
   D. All of the above.

6. _____ Which of the following is *not* an example of a proprietary credit card issuer?
   A. Target
   B. ExxonMobil
   C. Visa
   D. Sears

7. _____ The three Cs of credit are character, capacity, and _____.
   A. consumer
   B. cash
   C. co-signer
   D. capital

8. _____ The movement of money into and out of a business is _____.
   A. cash flow
   B. capacity
   C. collateral
   D. capital

9. _____ Property that a business uses to secure a loan is _____.
   A. capital
   B. conditions
   C. collateral
   D. cash flow

10. _____ Supplier financing and banking financing are two types of _____.
    A. open-end credit
    B. business credit
    C. installment loans
    D. unsecured credit

Completion

Choose the word(s) that best completes each of the following statements.

1. A loan for a specific amount that must be repaid with interest by a specified date or according to a specified schedule is _____ credit.

   _____

2. A loan for a specific amount of money that is repaid with interest in regular installments is a(n) _____ loan.

   _____

Name _____

3. A schedule that shows the amount of interest and principal for each payment so a loan can be repaid within a specific period of time is a(n) _____.

_____

4. The _____ is the annual cost of credit charged by a lender.

_____

5. A(n) _____ credit card is one that can only be used in the stores of the company that issued it.

_____

6. A credit score is also known as a(n) _____ score.

_____

7. A list of the individuals or businesses that owe money to a company is the _____.

_____

8. _____ is the owners' investment in a business.

_____

9. _____ is the ability of a business to repay a loan.

_____

10. Credit extended by a business to another business is called _____ credit.

_____

Part 2: Concept Review

Open Response

Respond to each of the following statements or questions. Use complete sentences.

1. What are four benefits provided by credit? Explain the risks of using credit.

   _____

   _____

   _____

   _____

   _____

   _____

   _____

2. What is the advantage of using the annual percentage rate (APR) to measure the annual cost of credit charged by a lender?

   _____

   _____

   _____

   _____

   _____

   _____

3. What are the potential benefits to a business of extending customer credit? What are the potential costs?

   _____

   _____

   _____

   _____

   _____

   _____

   _____

4. What is a credit policy? Identify the common elements of a credit policy.

_____

_____

_____

_____

_____

_____

_____

5. Establishing a good credit history makes it easier to obtain credit in the future. List the five factors that determine a FICO score. Explain how you can manage each of the factors to build and maintain a good credit score.

_____

_____

_____

_____

_____

_____

_____

_____

_____

_____

_____

Part 3: Math Skills

Interest

Credit is an agreement between two parties in which one party lends money or provides goods and services to another party with the understanding that payment will be made at a later date. Credit is not free. The total amount paid for credit includes interest and any fees. Interest is based on the amount borrowed, the interest rate, and the length of time of the loan. Simple interest is one formula that is used to calculate the interest cost of a loan:

$$P \times R \times T = \text{Interest}$$

Where: $P = $ Amount borrowed
$R = $ Interest rate
$T = $ Length of time of loan

The amount the borrower must repay when the loan is due is the amount borrowed plus the interest:

$$P + \text{Interest} = \text{Repayment Amount}$$

Answer the following questions involving interest.

1. Reynold borrows $15,000 to make improvements to a loading dock. The interest rate on the loan is 8 percent. The term of the loan is one year, during which time Reynold repays the amount borrowed plus interest. What is the interest on the loan? What is the repayment amount?

_____

_____

_____

2. Marc Jones borrows $5,000 on the business credit line to purchase raw materials. The loan plus interest is repaid after three months, or 3/12 of one year. The interest rate on the credit line is 6 percent. What is the interest charge? What is the amount that is repaid?

_____

_____

_____

3. Jeanne Smith normally uses a business credit line to purchase supplies for a printing business. The interest rate on this line is 10 percent. A supplier offers a special deal where $20,000 of supplies will be shipped, but no payment is due for six months, or 6/12 of one year. The supplier will not charge interest. How much interest will Jeanne save by purchasing from this supplier?

_____

_____

_____

4. RJ Industries ships $50,000 of merchandise to a customer. RJ allows the customer to pay the bill within one month with no interest due. Interest is charged on any balance remaining after one month at a 5 percent annual interest rate. The customer pays $10,000 after one month, and the remaining $40,000 after the second month. How much interest does RJ charge the customer?

_____

_____

_____

5. Refer to the previous problem. The customer tells RJ that it will only purchase the $50,000 of merchandise if it can repay after three months with no interest due. RJ agrees because it does not want to lose the sale. How much interest will RJ lose compared to its normal policy?

_____

_____

_____

Part 4: Communication Skills

Writing

Analogies can be very helpful when making presentations to customers. An *analogy* is a comparison of two things based on their being alike in some way, though dissimilar in every other way.

Section I

The following is a list of incomplete analogies. Provide the word that completes each analogy.

1. *Open* is to *close* as *near* is to _____.

   _____

2. *Clothes* is to *closet* as *car* is to _____.

   _____

3. *Lemon* is to *sour* as *candy* is to _____.

   _____

4. *Referee* is to basketball as *umpire* is to _____.

   _____

5. *Team* is to *play* as *crowd* is to _____.

   _____

6. *Bird* is to *fly* as a *fish* is to _____.

   _____

7. *Meow* is to *cat* as *bark* is to _____.

   _____

8. *Sun* is to *day* as *moon* is to _____.

   _____

9. *Knife* is to *cut* as *pen* is to _____.

   _____

10. *Son* is to *father* as *daughter* is to _____.

   _____

Section II

Next, create ten of your own analogies.

11. _____

   _____

12. _____

   _____

13. _____

   _____

14. _____
_____

15. _____
_____

16. _____
_____

17. _____
_____

18. _____
_____

19. _____
_____

20. _____
_____

CHAPTER 17 / Financial Management

Part 1: Content Review

Matching

Choose the letter of the correct term for each definition.

Terms:

A. financial planning
B. financial management
C. audit
D. budget
E. payroll

F. journal
G. accounting cycle
H. balance sheet
I. income statement
J. working capital

1. _____ A financial plan that reflects anticipated revenue and shows how it will be allocated in the operation of the business.

2. _____ A review of the financial statements of a business and the accounting practices that were used to produce them.

3. _____ A process used to manage the financial resources of a business.

4. _____ The sequence of steps businesses follow to record, summarize, and report financial information.

5. _____ Reports the revenue and expenses of a business for a specific time period and shows a net income or net loss.

6. _____ The difference between current assets and current liabilities of a business.

7. _____ A form used to record business transactions in chronological order.

8. _____ The process of setting financial goals and developing plans to reach them.

9. _____ A list of all employees working for the business and their earnings, benefits, taxes withheld, and other deductions.

10. _____ Reports the assets, liabilities, and owner's equity.

Multiple Choice

Choose the letter of the correct answer to each question.

1. _____ The system of recording business transactions and analyzing, verifying, and reporting the results is _____.
   A. auditing
   B. accounting
   C. financial statement analysis
   D. start-up budgeting

2. _____ The accounting equation is _____.
   A. assets + liabilities = owner's equity
   B. assets + owner's equity = liabilities
   C. assets = liabilities + owner's equity
   D. liabilities – owner's equity = assets

3. _____ Which of the following is *not* a paycheck withholding?
   A. gross pay
   B. FICA taxes
   C. income taxes
   D. employee benefits

4. _____ Records that prove a business transaction occurred are _____.
   A. journals
   B. special journals
   C. charts of account
   D. source documents

5. _____ Transferring information from journals to the ledger is _____.
   A. auditing
   B. budgeting
   C. posting
   D. journalizing

6. _____ One of the core goals of successful businesses is to _____.
   A. decrease working capital
   B. provide a return for investors
   C. increase the operating ratio
   D. All of the above.

7. _____ Projections of future business transactions are reported on _____.
   A. pro forma statements
   B. cash flow statements
   C. income statements
   D. audited statements

8. _____ Which of the following is an example of a current asset?
   A. Cash
   B. Inventory
   C. Accounts receivable
   D. All of the above.

9. _____ A(n) _____ reports how cash moves into and out of a business.
   A. general ledger
   B. income statement
   C. cash flow statement
   D. pro forma statement

10. _____ The _____ ratio shows the relationship of expenses to sales.
    A. net profit
    B. operating
    C. debt
    D. current

Completion

Choose the word(s) that best completes each of the following statements.

1. The period of time for which a business summarizes accounting information and prepares financial statements is a(n) _____.

   _____

2. The _____ is the projected sales units and revenue dollars for the period.

   _____

3. A(n) _____ budget is created in the planning stages of a new business.

_____

4. Recording the debit and credit parts of a transaction is called _____.

_____

5. A(n) _____ is a transaction for which cash for the sale is received at a later date.

_____

6. The amount of income earned before taxes and other deductions is _____.

_____

7. An amount of income that is not subject to income taxes is a(n) _____.

_____

8. Cash or any asset that will be exchanged for cash or used within one year is a(n) _____.

_____

9. A short-term debt that must be paid within one year is a(n) _____.

_____

10. The _____ statement summarizes changes in the owner's equity during a fiscal period.

_____

Part 2: Concept Review

Open Response

Respond to each of the following statements or questions. Use complete sentences.

1. What are generally accepted accounting principles (GAAP)? Why is it important for businesses to follow GAAP?

   _____

   _____

   _____

   _____

   _____

   _____

2. What is the difference between cash-basis accounting and accrual-basis accounting? Which method do most businesses use?

   _____

   _____

   _____

   _____

   _____

   _____

   _____

   _____

3. What is the purpose of financial statements? Who uses them?

   _____

   _____

   _____

   _____

   _____

Name _____

4. What are financial ratios? What information do financial ratios provide to business owners?

_____

_____

_____

_____

_____

_____

_____

5. The following table has financial data for two competing retailers of camping supplies. For each retailer, calculate the current ratio, debt ratio, net profit ratio, and operating ratio. Which company is bigger in terms of sales and assets? Which company do you think is performing better?

Financial Categories	Big Sky Camping Supplies	Great Outdoors Camping
Current Assets	$53,000	$245,000
Current Liabilities	19,000	169,000
Total Liabilities	105,000	789,500
Total Assets	168,000	1,035,800
Sales	212,000	578,900
Expenses	157,000	493,000
Net Income	55,000	85,000

Goodheart-Willcox Publisher

_____

_____

_____

_____

_____

_____

_____

Part 3: Math Skills

Number Sense

Business people need to have good number sense. *Number sense* is the ability to use and understand numbers to make judgments and solve problems. A person with good number sense also understands when personal computations are reasonable in the context of a problem.

Answer the following questions using good number sense.

1. A restaurant owner is looking to purchase new kitchen equipment and has a budget of $5,000 to spend. An oven is priced at $2,100, a freezer at $1,200, and an automatic toaster at $350. Without using a calculator, what is the total for all three items? Will this be within budget?

   _____

   _____

2. You are installing cabinetry to fit a space that is 60 inches wide. This measurement needs to be converted from inches to feet to estimate the cost of the cabinets. You use a calculator to divide 60 by 12 (number of inches in a foot). The answer displayed is 720. Is this answer correct? Explain your answer.

   _____

   _____

3. Good number sense is needed for those who handle money regularly, such as retail cashiers. Cashiers often use a register that scans the barcode of each item to find its price. A customer checks out with three gallons of milk, two boxes of cereal, and four cans of tuna. None of the items are price marked, but you know that a gallon of milk is always priced at $2.99. You scan each item and the total price of $9.79 appears on the cash register monitor. Does this total seem reasonable to you? Explain your answer.

   _____

   _____

   _____

4. You are tire shopping for your delivery vehicle and visit two tire stores. Quality Tires will install the tires you need for $200 each. The same installed tires at Discount Wheels are $250 each. However, Discount Wheels is advertising that when you buy three tires, the fourth is free. Which tire store has the better buy? Explain your answer.

   _____

   _____

   _____

5. You want to buy a package of turkey jerky. A four-ounce package is priced at $2.00. A one-pound package is priced at $6.29. Which size is the better value for the money? Explain your answer.

   _____

   _____

   _____

Part 4: Communication Skills

Reading

Writers tailor their writing specifically for audiences and situations. Read the passage below and focus on the content. After you have read the passage, answer the questions that follow.

Substance Abuse Policy

The Marco Company is committed to programs that promote the health and safety of our employees in the workplace and protect our business from unnecessary loss. Consistent with the spirit and intent of this commitment, the Company promotes a drug-free environment and has adopted this substance abuse policy regarding the sale, use, possession, or distribution by its employees of alcohol or chemical substances that may induce dependence or addiction. As a condition of your employment, you are required to abide by this policy. It is a serious violation of Company policy for any employee of the Company in any location or on Company business anywhere:

- to possess, use, sell, offer to sell, or distribute alcoholic beverages, except in cases of company-sponsored functions where the Company can control and monitor the use of alcohol;
- to possess, use, sell, offer to sell, or distribute any illegal drugs or any drugs that have been legally obtained but are used for anything other than their legally intended purpose;
- to be under the influence of alcohol to the point where it impedes your ability to work, drive, interact respectfully with others, or otherwise exhibit satisfactory work performance, motor skills, or speech;
- to be under the influence of illegal drugs;
- to misuse or abuse any drug or other substance, whether legal or illegal.

It is the employee's responsibility to seek diagnosis and treatment for alcohol or drug use before it becomes a disciplinary matter. This substance abuse policy applies to all applicants and employees of the Company. Illegal drug usage and/or chemical dependency and alcohol usage or dependency will not be tolerated.

Reading Questions

1. Who is the writer of this passage?

   _____

   _____

   _____

2. What is the writer's purpose?

   _____

   _____

   _____

   _____

3. Does the writer expect something from the reader? If so, what is it?

   _____

   _____

   _____

   _____

   _____

Notes

_____

_____

_____

_____

_____

_____

_____

_____

_____

_____

_____

_____

_____

_____

_____

_____

_____

_____

_____

_____

_____

_____

_____

_____

_____

_____

_____

_____

CHAPTER 18 / Income and Taxes

Part 1: Content Review

Matching

Choose the letter of the correct term for each definition.

Terms:

A. personal financial management
B. earned income
C. minimum wage
D. net pay
E. FICA taxes

F. tax return
G. taxable income
H. payroll deduction
I. standard deduction
J. tax liability

1. _____ A report containing information used to calculate taxes owed by a taxpayer.

2. _____ Taxes paid by the employee and employer that are used to finance the federal Social Security and Medicare programs.

3. _____ Dollar amount that non-itemizers may subtract from their income before income tax is applied.

4. _____ The lowest hourly wage employers can pay most workers by law.

5. _____ Subtraction from gross pay.

6. _____ Process used by individuals to manage limited income to meet personal unlimited needs and wants.

7. _____ Gross pay minus payroll deductions.

8. _____ The amount on which taxes are calculated.

9. _____ Income received from employment or from self-employment.

10. _____ Tax owed on total income for a year.

Multiple Choice

Choose the letter of the correct answer to each question.

1. _____ Personal financial management begins when someone _____ money.
   A. receives
   B. spends
   C. borrows
   D. inherits

2. _____ The amount paid for working beyond the 40-hour work week is _____.
   A. net pay
   B. regular pay
   C. overtime wage
   D. earned income

3. _____ A subtraction from gross pay is a(n) _____.
   A. standard deduction
   B. itemized deduction
   C. payroll deduction
   D. tax deduction

4. _____ FICA taxes include _____.
   A. federal and state taxes
   B. state and Social Security taxes
   C. standard and itemized deductions
   D. Social Security and Medicare taxes

5. _____ Which of the following is a basic step in the budget process?
   A. Set a budget period
   B. List estimated income
   C. List estimated expenses
   D. All of the above.

6. _____ A(n) _____ occurs if more money is spent than budgeted.
   A. unfavorable variance
   B. favorable variance
   C. fixed expense
   D. variable expense

7. _____ A statement that shows earnings and tax deductions withheld during the years is a _____.
   A. Form 1040
   B. Form W-4
   C. Form W-2 Wage and Tax Statement
   D. Form 1040-SR

8. _____ Which is *not* an example of earned income?
   A. Wages
   B. Interest
   C. Tips
   D. Commission

9. _____ All of the following are examples of unearned income *except* _____.
   A. bonuses
   B. Social Security income
   C. rental income
   D. lottery winnings

10. _____ Eligible workers who work overtime hours earn at least _____ times their regular hours.
    A. 1 1/2
    B. 2
    C. 2 1/2
    D. 3

Completion

Choose the word(s) that best completes each of the following statements.

1. _____ means having the ability to understand basic topics related to finance.

   _____

2. _____ means that the government expects individuals and businesses to voluntarily report all income subject to the income tax.

   _____

3. Income received from employment or from self-employment is ____.

_____

4. Money paid for service beyond the payment that is required is a(n) ____.

_____

5. A subtraction from gross pay is a(n) ____.

_____

6. A(n) ____ is an expense that can go up or down during the budget period.

_____

7. Earnings from sources other than work is ____.

_____

8. The dollar amount that non-itemizers may subtract from their income tax depending on their filing status is called a(n) ____.

_____

9. An amount of ____ is found on tax tables available on the IRS website.

_____

10. The ____ is an IRS service that offers free tax help to lower-income people who need assistance in preparing their tax returns.

_____

Part 2: Concept Review

Open Response

Respond to each of the following statements or questions. Use complete sentences.

1. Explain how trade-offs and opportunity costs apply to personal financial management.

_____

_____

_____

_____

_____

_____

_____

_____

2. Earned income is income received from employment or self-employment. List three types of earned income and briefly describe each.

_____

_____

_____

_____

_____

_____

3. What is a personal budget? What are the basic steps in the budget process?

_____

_____

_____

_____

_____

_____

_____

_____

Name _____

4. Why is it important to provide accurate information on a tax return form?

_____

_____

_____

_____

_____

_____

5. A friend must a file an income tax return for the first time and needs some assistance. Identify sources that are available for tax planning information and assistance that your friend can use to complete the tax return.

_____

_____

_____

_____

_____

_____

_____

_____

Part 3: Math Skills

Mixed Mathematics

Employees need to understand how their payroll checks are prepared. In general, withholdings are deducted from an employee's gross pay. Gross pay is the amount of earnings before taxes and other deductions are withheld. Payroll deductions include FICA taxes for Social Security and Medicare, employee benefits, and federal, state, and local taxes. Net pay is gross pay minus payroll deductions. It is also known as take-home pay.

net pay = gross pay – payroll deductions

Connor earns a $60,000 annual salary, which is paid bimonthly. The current Social Security tax for employees is 6.2% on the first $118,500 of gross pay. The employee Medicare tax is 1.45% on all gross pay. In addition, Connor's employer withholds 10% of gross pay for federal tax and 5% for state tax. Finally, 4% of gross pay is withheld as a contribution to an employee saving plan. The deduction for health insurance is $200 for each pay period. Calculate the net pay Connor will take home in each bimonthly paycheck.

$60,000 annual gross pay ÷ 24 payments = $2,500 bimonthly gross pay
Social Security Tax: $2,500 × .062 = $155
Medicare Tax: $2,500 × .0145 = $36.25
Federal Tax: $2,500 × .10 = $250
State Tax: $2,500 × .05 = $125
Savings Plan: $2,500 × .04 = $100
Health Insurance = $200
gross pay – payroll deductions = net pay
$2,500 – $155 – $36.25 – $250 – $125 – $100 – $200 = $1,633.75

Answer the following questions about calculating pay.

1. Adam earns a $35,000 annual salary, which is paid weekly. The current Social Security tax for employees is 6.2% on the first $118,500 of gross pay. The employee Medicare tax is 1.45% on all gross pay. In addition, Adam's employer deducts 10% of the week's gross pay for federal tax and 3% for state tax. Finally, the deduction for health insurance is $70 for each pay period. Calculate the net pay that Adam will take home in each weekly paycheck.

2. Refer to the previous problem. Adam receives a $5,000 annual pay raise. Calculate the new net pay. Assume there are no changes in withholding rates.

3. Cassandra starts a new position in a company with a gross pay of $52,000, which is paid weekly. The current Social Security tax for employees is 6.2% on the first $118,500 of gross pay. The employee Medicare tax is 1.45% on all gross pay. Cassandra's employer deducts 10% of the gross pay for federal tax, but there is no state tax. The health insurance contribution is $60 a week. Calculate Cassandra's net pay.

_____

_____

_____

_____

_____

Many employees earn an hourly wage. In this case, gross pay is calculated as follows:

$$gross\ pay = hourly\ wage \times hours\ worked$$

If hourly workers work more than 40 hours per week, they must receive overtime pay of at least 1 1/2 times their regular hourly wage for all overtime hours. The formula for overtime (OT) wages is as follows:

$$OT\ hourly\ wage = hourly\ wage \times 1.5$$
$$total\ OT\ wages = OT\ hourly\ wage \times OT\ hours$$

Total OT wages are then added to the employee's regular pay for 40 hours of work to determine gross pay:

$$gross\ pay = regular\ pay + total\ OT\ wages$$

Gordon earns $10 an hour and worked 45 hours last week. Gross pay is calculated as follows:

Regular pay = $10 × 40 hours = $400
$10 × 1.5 = $15 OT hourly wage
$15 × 5 = $75 OT wages
$400 + $75 = $475 gross pay

4. Larson earns $19.75 per hour, works 40 hours, and is paid weekly. The current Social Security tax for employees is 6.2% on the first $118,500 of gross pay. The employee Medicare tax is 1.45% on all gross pay. In addition, Larson's employer deducts 9% of the gross pay for federal tax, 4.5% for state tax, and 1.0% for local tax. 4% of gross pay is withheld as a contribution to an employee saving plan. The weekly withholding for health insurance is $65. Calculate Larson's net pay.

_____

_____

_____

_____

_____

5. Refer to the previous problem. Larson worked 50 hours last week. Calculate the week's net pay.

_____

_____

_____

_____

_____

_____

Part 4: Communication Skills

Writing

Writing skills are crucial in effective communication. When written material includes numbers, it is important to be watchful and consistent to avoid costly errors. Edit the following paragraph. Insert proper punctuation, correct misspelled words and grammar errors, and rewrite sentences to improve the structure, as needed.

Thank you for asking green lights inc. to bid on the instalation and maintenance of an energy-efficient lighting system for your new branch office. after carefully reviewing the specifications you provided we had our electricians conduct a therow on-site survey of your new office. Our bid team used the electricians evaluations along with your specs to create an estimate for this job. We are projecting the complete instalation cost to be 5575. This is a one time charge payable upon satisfactory completion of the work. For you're convenience, i am attaching a detailed proposal. This proposal includes an option for us to handle full maintenance, for 5 years at a cost of one hundred seventy-five a year for a full-inspection, plus the cost of any repaire or replacement needs identified in the course of the inspection. Thank you, again for the oportunity to submit this bid. Please let me know if you would like to discus our proposal before making your decision.

CHAPTER 19 Personal Banking and Investments

Part 1: Content Review

Matching

Choose the letter of the correct term for each definition.

Terms:

A. savings plan
B. overdraft
C. money order
D. payee
E. bank statement

F. money market account (MMA)
G. investing
H. diversification
I. mutual fund
J. estate

1. _____ A record of checks, ATM transactions, deposits, and charges on an account.

2. _____ The person, business, or organization to whom a check is written.

3. _____ Purchasing a financial product or valuable item with the goal of increasing wealth over time in spite of possible loss.

4. _____ The process of spreading risk by putting money in a variety of investments.

5. _____ A check written for an amount greater than the balance of the account.

6. _____ Consists of the assets and liabilities a person leaves after death.

7. _____ An investment created by pooling the money of many people and investing it in a collection of securities.

8. _____ A type of savings account that requires a higher minimum balance than a regular savings account, but offers a higher interest rate.

9. _____ A strategy for using money to reach important goals and to advance financial security.

10. _____ A payment order for a specific amount of money payable to a specific payee.

Multiple Choice

Choose the letter of the correct answer to each question.

1. _____ Using a debit card has the same result as _____.
   A. using a credit card
   B. writing a check
   C. borrowing money
   D. saving money

2. _____ Which of the following is an example of a banking service?
   A. Safe-deposit box
   B. Loan
   C. Special payment service
   D. All of the above.

3. _____ Which of the following is *not* required to open a checking account?
   A. Credit report
   B. Signature
   C. Personal identification
   D. Social Security number

4. _____ When a customer has _____, a financial institution will honor a check even if it exceeds the account balance.
   A. a stop-payment order
   B. been loyal
   C. overdraft protection service
   D. many accounts

5. _____ Reconciling a bank statement means comparing the _____.
   A. check register to the checking account
   B. check register to the savings account
   C. savings account to the checking account
   D. credit card to the debit card

6. _____ A _____ requires a fixed deposit amount for a fixed period of time.
   A. basic savings account
   B. high-yield savings account
   C. money market account (MMA)
   D. certificate of deposit (CD)

7. _____ The portion of a company's earnings that is paid to stockholders is a(n) _____.
   A. interest payment
   B. dividend
   C. annuity
   D. deposit

8. _____ A(n) _____ is a contract with an insurance company that provides regular income for a set period of time, usually for life.
   A. 401(k)
   B. 403(b)
   C. Roth IRA
   D. annuity

9. _____ A retirement program can be sponsored or started by _____.
   A. employers
   B. individuals
   C. the self-employed
   D. All of the above.

10. _____ A legal document stating a person's wishes for an estate after death is a(n) _____.
    A. will
    B. estate plan
    C. annuity
    D. Keogh plan

Completion

Choose the word(s) that best completes each of the following statements.

1. A(n) _____ is a bank account that allows the owner to make deposits, write checks, and withdraw money.

_____

2. A(n) _____ is a card that allows the user to electronically access account funds at an ATM and to pay for purchases from a business.

_____

Name _____

3. A bank account used by depositors to accumulate money for future use is a(n) _____.

   _____

4. A payment order for a specific amount of money payable to a specific payee is a(n) _____.

   _____

5. A combination savings and checking account is a(n) _____ checking account.

   _____

6. The signature on the back of a check is a(n) _____.

   _____

7. A plan to develop investment growth is a(n) _____ plan.

   _____

8. A(n) _____ is a collection of securities and other assets a person owns.

   _____

9. Objects purchased for the pleasure of ownership and because they are expected to increase in value are _____.

   _____

10. An individual retirement account in which individuals contribute after-tax income and qualified withdrawals are not taxed is a(n) _____.

   _____

Part 2: Concept Review

Open Response

Respond to each of the following statements or questions. Use complete sentences.

1. You are making a large purchase and offer to pay with a personal check. The seller insists on a cashier's check or certified check. Why do you think this is the case?

_____

_____

_____

_____

_____

2. What potential problem might occur if the balance in your check register does *not* match the balance in your checking account?

_____

_____

_____

_____

_____

3. Identify four different types of savings accounts. What are three factors that distinguish these types of accounts from each another?

_____

_____

_____

_____

_____

4. What is the difference between a traditional IRA and a Roth IRA?

_____

_____

_____

_____

_____

5. Credit and debit cards are very popular and widely used to make purchases. Compare the advantages and disadvantages of credit and debit cards.

_____

_____

_____

_____

_____

_____

_____

Part 3: Math Skills

Adding, Subtracting, Multiplying, and Dividing Fractions

Businesses often use fractions in their business activities. A fraction is a part of a whole. It is made of a numerator that is divided by a denominator:

$$\frac{\text{Numerator}}{\text{Denominator}}$$

The numerator specifies the number of equal parts that are in the fraction. The denominator shows how many equal parts make up the whole. In a proper fraction, the numerator is less than the denominator. An *improper fraction* is a fraction where the numerator is equal to or greater than the denominator. A *mixed number* contains a whole number and a fraction.

Answer the following problems involving fractions.

1. Fractions must often be added. To add fractions, the numerators are combined and the denominators stay the same. If possible, simplify your answer to the smallest possible fraction.

   Bounty Best Foods makes a fruit salad that includes 3/8 pound of grapes, 1/8 pound of mandarin oranges, and 3/8 pound of cherries. What is the total weight of the fruit salad?

   _____

   _____

2. Fractions must have a common denominator in order to be added. When the denominators are different, the fractions must first be converted so the denominators are the same. In some cases, this means calculating the *least common denominators*. To find the least common denominator, list multiples of each denominator and then identify the smallest common value. Once you have the least common denominator, determine what number is multiplied by the denominator to achieve the least common denominator and multiple the numerator by the same number for each fraction. Once all fractions have the same denominator, add the numerators and simplify the answer. For example, to add 1/2 and 1/4, first convert 1/2 to 2/4. The least common denominator is 4, so 1/2 must be multiplied by 2 so that both fractions have the same denominator.

   Bounty Best Foods makes a bean salad that combines 3/8 pound of green beans with 1/2 pound of wax beans.

   A. What is the least common denominator?

   _____

   B. What is the total weight of the bean salad?

   _____

   _____

3. To subtract fractions, the second numerator is subtracted from the first numerator. The denominators stay the same. Fractions can only be subtracted when they have a common denominator. Use the process described in the previous question to find a common denominator. Simplify your answer.

   Green Acres Landscaping prepares a lawn seed mixture consisting of 7/8 pound of perennial ryegrass and 3/8 pound of fine fescue. How much more ryegrass is used than fine fescue?

   _____

   _____

4. Common denominators are not necessary when multiplying fractions. Multiply all of the numerators and multiply all of the denominators. Once completed, simplify the fraction if possible.

Green Acres Landscaping prepares a liquid fertilizer spray using 3/8 cup of a nitrogen fertilizer with one gallon of water. How much nitrogen fertilizer should be mixed with only 1/2 of a gallon of water?

_____

_____

5. To divide one fraction by a second fraction, multiply the first fraction by the *reciprocal* of the second fraction. The reciprocal of a fraction is created by switching the numerator and denominator. As always, simplify your answer to the smallest possible fraction.

Green Acres Landscaping has 5/8 gallon of plant nutrient to fertilize its customers' flower beds. Each flower bed needs 1/8 gallon of nutrient. How many flower beds can be fertilized?

_____

_____

Part 4: Communication Skills

Speaking

An *idiom* is a phrase that is not taken literally, but has a special meaning that is common to a culture. For example, when you "give someone a hand," it means you give them applause and not a part of your body. Idioms should be avoided in formal business communication. However, they can have a positive impact on your message in less formal situations.

Provide the meaning of each of the following idioms.

1. A piece of cake.

   _____

2. Let the cat out of the bag.

   _____

3. Feel under the weather.

   _____

4. Down in the dumps.

   _____

5. Speak of the devil.

   _____

6. It cost an arm and leg.

   _____

7. Jump the gun.

   _____

8. Don't jump all over me.

   _____

9. Raining cats and dogs.

   _____

10. You're pulling my leg.

   _____

11. Let me sleep on it.

   _____

12. You're wet behind the ears.

   _____

13. When pigs fly.

   _____

14. Let's shoot the breeze.

   _____

15. Cut corners.

   _____

CHAPTER 20 Insurance

Part 1: Content Review

Matching

Choose the letter of the correct term for each definition.

Terms:

A. coinsurance

B. preauthorization

C. regular medical insurance

D. copayment

E. beneficiary

F. term life insurance

G. umbrella policy

H. depreciation

I. bodily injury liability

J. no-fault auto insurance

1. _____ Insurance coverage that protects a person who is responsible for an auto accident that results in the injury or death of other parties.

2. _____ An insurance policy that covers loss amounts that are higher than those covered by primary policies.

3. _____ A person or organization named by a policyholder to receive the death benefit of an insurance policy after the policyholder's death.

4. _____ A flat fee the patient must pay for medical services.

5. _____ An approval from an insurance plan before receiving certain procedures and treatments.

6. _____ A type of insurance that provides protection only for a specific period of time.

7. _____ A decrease in the value of property as a result of age or wear and tear.

8. _____ Insurance coverage which includes prescriptions, hospital stays, and inpatient tests.

9. _____ A type of insurance plan that eliminates the fault-finding process in settling claims.

10. _____ A percentage of the service costs that patients pay.

Multiple Choice

Choose the letter of the correct answer to each question.

1. _____ Risks that affect personal or real property are _____.
   A. exclusions
   B. personal risks
   C. property risks
   D. liability risks

2. _____ Risks resulting from the possibility of losing money or other property as a result of legal proceedings are _____.
   A. exclusions
   B. personal risks
   C. property risks
   D. liability risks

3. _____ The process of measuring risk and finding ways to minimize risk is _____.
   A. risk management
   B. utilization review
   C. coinsurance
   D. copayment

4. _____ Which of the following is *not* a form of managed care?
   A. Health maintenance organization (HMO)
   B. Children's Health Insurance Program (CHIP)
   C. Preferred provider organization (PPO)
   D. Point-of-service plan (POS)

5. _____ Government-sponsored health care for eligible citizens age 65 and older is _____.
   A. Medicaid
   B. Medicare
   C. Social Security
   D. umbrella coverage

6. _____ Which of the following is a type of whole life insurance?
   A. Term life
   B. Variable life
   C. Endowment life
   D. All of the above.

7. _____ Insurance that covers damage to property and offers liability protection is _____.
   A. homeowners insurance
   B. no-fault insurance
   C. coinsurance
   D. comprehensive coverage

8. _____ Which of the following would *not* be covered under a health insurance policy?
   A. Medical expenses resulting from auto accident
   B. Car damage from accident or collision
   C. Injury caused by uninsured or hit-and-run driver
   D. All of the above.

9. _____ Auto insurance premiums tend to be higher for young, single males because they _____.
   A. drive more expensive cars
   B. choose higher deductibles
   C. tend to have more accidents
   D. choose lower coverage amounts

10. _____ Increasing the deductible amount for auto insurance will _____.
    A. reduce premiums
    B. increase premiums
    C. increase the liability coverage
    D. reduce the liability coverage

Completion

Choose the word(s) that best completes each of the following statements.

1. The process of measuring risk and finding ways to minimize or manage loss is _____.

   _____

2. A(n) _____ is an amount of money regularly paid to an insurance company for a policy.

   _____

3. A medical service that is not covered under an insurance plan is a(n) _____.

   _____

4. A percentage of medical costs that a patient pays is _____.

_____

5. _____ medical insurance combines basic and major medical protection in one policy.

_____

6. A government health insurance program for eligible low-income persons and those with certain disabilities is _____.

_____

7. _____ insurance pays a portion of income lost to a worker who is unable to work for a prolonged period due to a non-work related illness or injury.

_____

8. A type of life insurance that provides basic lifetime protection, as long as premiums are paid, is _____ insurance.

_____

9. Homeowners insurance provides two basic types of coverage: property protection and _____.

_____

10. Auto insurance coverage that protects a person who is responsible for an auto accident that results in the injury or death of other parties is _____.

_____

Part 2: Concept Review

Open Response

Respond to each of the following statements or questions. Use complete sentences.

1. Identify five types of health insurance plans. Briefly explain the coverage provided by each.

   _____

   _____

   _____

   _____

   _____

   _____

   _____

   _____

   _____

   _____

2. What is a managed care plan? What is the biggest advantage of a managed care plan? What is the biggest disadvantage?

   _____

   _____

   _____

   _____

   _____

   _____

3. What is life insurance? Who is protected by life insurance?

   _____

   _____

   _____

   _____

   _____

   _____

Name _____

4. Homeowners insurance provides two basic types of coverage: property protection and liability protection. Explain the difference between property and liability protection.

_____

_____

_____

_____

_____

5. What are the major factors that determine the cost of auto insurance? List four ways you can attempt to reduce auto insurance premiums.

_____

_____

_____

_____

_____

_____

_____

_____

_____

_____

Part 3: Math Skills

Rounding

Math is a practical tool to solve problems and make decisions. Sometimes, precise calculations or measurements are not needed and it is easier to work with rounded numbers. When a number is *rounded*, some of the digits are changed, removed, or changed to zero. For example, if you are calculating millions of dollars, it might not be important to know the amount down to the single dollar or cent. Instead, you might round the amount to the nearest ten thousand or even hundred thousand dollars. To round a number, follow these steps:

- Underline the digit in the place to which you are rounding.
- If the digit to the right of this place is 5 or greater, add 1 to the underlined digit.
- If the digit to the right is less than 5, do *not* add 1 to the underlined digit.
- Change all the digits to the right of the underlined digit to zero.

Answer the following questions that involve rounding.

1. The revenue for Vance Medical Supplies was $2,359,774.18 last year. The accountant at Vance Medical is preparing its financial statements, which use numbers rounded to the nearest thousand dollars. What revenue figure will appear in the financial statements?

   _____

2. The chief financial officer (CFO) of B-Well Drug Stores is preparing a presentation to the Board of Directors. The CFO wants to graph the growth of annual sales over the last five years, from 2017 to 2021, by rounding the sales numbers to the nearest hundred thousand dollars. What sales numbers will be used in the graph?

   A. 2021: $13,168,499

   _____

   B. 2020: $12,447,885

   _____

   C. 2019: $12,884,116

   _____

   D. 2018: $12,036,381

   _____

   E. 2017: $11,611,449

   _____

3. The utility expense for Ryan Storage was $32,365.55 last year. You are preparing a budget for next year which will use numbers rounded to the nearest thousand dollars. How much is the rounded amount of last year's utility expense?

   _____

4. Round the following prices to the indicated amount:

   A. $5.77 to the nearest dollar

   _____

   B. $39,992 to the nearest thousand

   _____

   C. $92.19 to the nearest ten dollars

   _____

D. $33,561,833 to the nearest million

_____

E. $599 to the nearest hundred

_____

5. Last year, the sales of Garrett Sports, an online retailer, were $15,145,890. As Garrett's purchasing manager, you attend a trade show to meet with potential suppliers. One of the suppliers wants to know if your company is a large volume retailer. Respond by giving last year's sales figure rounded to the nearest million.

_____

Part 4: Communication Skills

Reading

Reading skills are essential both in business and in managing your personal life. The ability to read through text and determine important information is a skill necessary in making informed decisions and plans. Read the passage below and focus on the content. After you have read the passage, answer the questions that follow.

COBRA

Congress passed the landmark Consolidated Omnibus Budget Reconciliation Act (COBRA) health benefit provisions in 1986. COBRA contains provisions giving certain former employees, retirees, spouses/former spouses, and dependent children the right to temporary continuation of health coverage at group rates. Employers with 20 or more employees are usually required to offer COBRA coverage and to notify their employees of the availability of such coverage. This coverage, however, is only available when coverage is lost due to certain specific events.

There are 3 elements to qualifying for COBRA benefits. COBRA establishes specific criteria for plans, qualified beneficiaries, and qualifying events: plan coverage, qualified beneficiaries, and qualifying events.

Plan Coverage. Group health plans for employers with 20 or more employees on more than 50 percent of its typical business days in the previous calendar year are subject to COBRA. Each part-time employee counts as a fraction of an employee, with the fraction equal to the number of hours that the part-time employee worked divided by the hours an employee must work to be considered full-time.

Qualified Beneficiaries. A qualified beneficiary is an individual covered by a group health plan on the day before a qualifying event; either an employee, an employee's spouse, or an employee's dependent child.

Qualifying Events. Qualifying events are certain events that would cause an individual to lose health coverage. The type of qualifying event determines who the qualified beneficiaries are and the amount of time that a plan must offer the health coverage to them under COBRA.

The qualifying events for employees are:

- Voluntary or involuntary termination of employment for any reason other than gross misconduct
- Reduction in the number of hours of employment

The qualifying events for spouses are:

- Voluntary or involuntary termination of the covered employee's employment for any reason other than gross misconduct
- Reduction in the hours worked by the covered employee
- Covered employee becoming entitled to Medicare
- Divorce or legal separation of the covered employee
- Death of the covered employee

The qualifying events for dependent children are the same as for the spouse with one addition:

- Loss of dependent child status under the plan rules

Beneficiaries may be required to pay for COBRA coverage. The premium cannot exceed 102 percent of the cost to the plan for similarly covered individuals who have not experienced a qualifying event. In general, qualified beneficiaries must be offered the same coverage they had immediately before qualifying for continuation coverage. Changes in benefits under the plan for active employees also apply to qualified COBRA beneficiaries.

The administration of COBRA is shared by three federal agencies. The U.S. Department of Labor handles questions about notification rights under COBRA for private-sector employees. The Department of Health and Human Services handles questions relating to state and local government workers. The Internal Revenue Service within the Department of the Treasury has other COBRA jurisdiction.

Source:
United States Department of Labor, Frequently Asked Questions: COBRA Continuation Health Coverage; www.dol.gov

Name _____

Reading Questions

1. What is the purpose of the Consolidated Omnibus Budget Reconciliation Act?

   _____

   _____

   _____

   _____

   _____

2. What is a qualifying event? What are the qualification criteria for employees?

   _____

   _____

   _____

   _____

   _____

3. Who handles the administration of COBRA?

   _____

   _____

   _____

   _____

Notes

CHAPTER 21 Career Planning

Part 1: Content Review

Matching

Choose the letter of the correct term for each definition.

Terms:

A. job
B. career
C. skill
D. ability
E. networking

F. internship
G. apprenticeship
H. certification
I. scholarship
J. work-study program

1. _____ A professional status earned by an individual after passing an exam focused on a specific body of knowledge.

2. _____ The mastery of a skill or the capacity to do something.

3. _____ Talking with people you know and making new contacts.

4. _____ Financial aid that may be based on financial need or some type of merit or accomplishment.

5. _____ A combination of on-the-job training, work experience, and classroom instruction.

6. _____ The work a person does regularly in order to earn money.

7. _____ Part-time jobs on a college campus.

8. _____ Something an individual does well.

9. _____ A short-term position with a sponsoring organization that gives an opportunity to gain on-the-job experience.

10. _____ A series of related jobs in the same profession.

Multiple Choice

Choose the letter of the correct answer to each question.

1. _____ Critical skills necessary to perform the required work-related tasks of a position are _____ skills.
   A. transferrable
   B. job-specific
   C. postsecondary
   D. career cluster

2. _____ The highest-level position on a career ladder is _____.
   A. executive
   B. supervisory
   C. specialist
   D. career-level

3. _____ A position on the career ladder that has management responsibility is _____.
   A. specialist
   B. certification
   C. supervisory
   D. career-level

4. _____ A list of steps on a time line to reach each of your career goals is a career _____.
   A. cluster
   B. plan
   C. ladder
   D. foundation

5. _____ Which of the following in an example of an aptitude?
   A. Mathematics
   B. Drawing
   C. Writing
   D. All of the above.

6. _____ Which of the following is an example of formal education?
   A. High school
   B. Two-year college
   C. Four-year college
   D. All of the above.

7. _____ Education that prepares you for a specific type of work is _____.
   A. formal education
   B. occupational training
   C. certification
   D. college access

8. _____ Students in postsecondary school choose a(n) _____ that suits an interest or meets a career goal.
   A. certification
   B. aptitude
   C. continuing education unit (CEU)
   D. area of study

9. _____ Which of the following sources of college funding must be repaid?
   A. Work-study
   B. Grant
   C. Scholarship
   D. Governmental education loan

10. _____ A 529 plan is a type of _____.
    A. career plan
    B. career pathway
    C. saving plan
    D. college curriculum

Completion

Choose the word(s) that best completes each of the following statements.

1. A(n) _____ position is usually a person's first or beginning job.

   _____

2. A(n) _____ position requires specialized knowledge and skills in a specific field.

   _____

3. A list of steps on a time line to reach each of your career goals is a(n) _____.

   _____

4. Taking a(n) _____ helps identify your aptitudes, abilities, values, and interests.

_____

5. The process of deciding what a person wants to achieve is _____.

_____

6. Any education received after high school is _____ education.

_____

7. A(n) _____ school is one that returns money it earns back into the school.

_____

8. _____ refers to building awareness about college opportunities, providing guidance regarding college admissions, and identifying ways to pay for college.

_____

9. A financial award that does not have to be repaid and is typically provided by a nonprofit organization is a(n) _____.

_____

10. Financial-aid awards available for students and families who meet certain economic requirements are _____.

_____

Part 2: Concept Review

Open Response

Respond to each of the following statements or questions. Use complete sentences.

1. What are employability skills? List four major types of employability skills.

   _____

   _____

   _____

   _____

   _____

2. What are values? How do values apply to career planning and success?

   _____

   _____

   _____

   _____

   _____

3. Identify four sources of career training for those who do not wish to attend college.

   _____

   _____

   _____

   _____

4. What is professional certification? Do you think it might be beneficial to earn a professional certification in your career field, even if your current employer does not require it? Briefly explain your answer.

   _____

   _____

   _____

   _____

   _____

   _____

   _____

5. Choose three potential sources of funding your college education. Identify the benefits and disadvantages of each.

_____

_____

_____

_____

_____

_____

_____

Part 3: Math Skills

Graphing

Data must often be organized and presented in way that makes it easier to understand, such as with a graph. Graphs are used to illustrate data in a picture-like format. Common types of graphs are bar graphs, line graphs, and circle graphs. A bar graph organizes information along a vertical axis and horizontal axis. The vertical axis runs up and down one side and lists data, such as sales figures. The horizontal axis runs along the bottom and typically indicates a time line. The following monthly sales data are illustrated in a bar graph that follows:

- June: $19,000
- July: $20,500
- August: $22,000
- September: $22,750
- October: $21,500

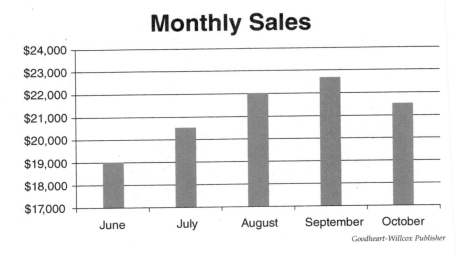

Goodheart-Willcox Publisher

A line graph also organizes information on a vertical and horizontal axis. However, data are graphed as a continuous line rather than a set of bars. Line graphs are often used to show trends over a period of time. The following line graph illustrates the previously mentioned monthly sales data.

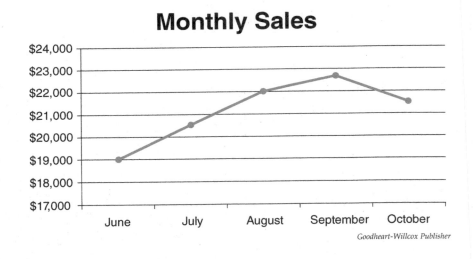

Goodheart-Willcox Publisher

A circle graph looks like a divided circle and shows how a whole object is cut into parts. Circle graphs are also called *pie charts* and are often used to illustrate percentages. The following data represent the percentage of a supermarket's sales contributed by its various departments and are illustrated in the circle graph that follows:

- Health and Beauty: 6 percent
- Grocery: 20 percent
- Produce: 20 percent
- Dairy: 24 percent
- Meat and Seafood: 30 percent

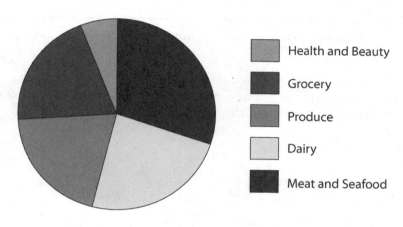

Percentages by Department

- Health and Beauty
- Grocery
- Produce
- Dairy
- Meat and Seafood

Goodheart-Willcox Publisher

Answer the following questions involving graphs.

1. The following data represent monthly sales from Midwest Pool Supplies. Create a bar graph to illustrate the data.
   - February: $12,000
   - March: $11,600
   - April: $16,500
   - May: $19,200
   - June: $24,500
   - July: $32,100
   - August: $14,500

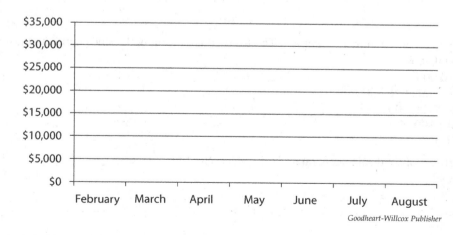

Goodheart-Willcox Publisher

2. Refer to the previous question. Create a line graph to illustrate the sales data.

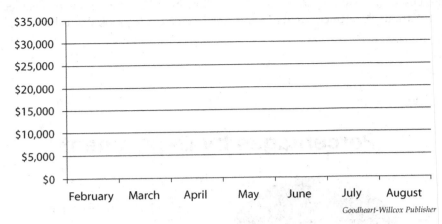

Goodheart-Willcox Publisher

3. Chet's Plumbing Supplies operates in five Midwestern states. The following data represent the percentage of total sales from each of these states. Create a circle graph to illustrate the data.
   - Michigan: 39 percent
   - Illinois: 30 percent
   - Indiana: 14 percent
   - Ohio: 11 percent
   - Wisconsin: 6 percent

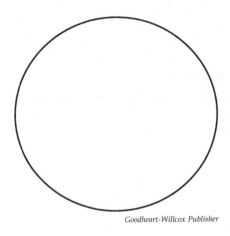

Goodheart-Willcox Publisher

4. Larry's Fun City is an entertainment complex. The following data show the sales generated last year from the four areas of its business.
   - Go-Carts: $210,000
   - Golf Driving Range: $180,000
   - Batting Cages: $120,000
   - Miniature Golf: $90,000
   - **Total:** $600,000

Calculate the percent of total sales generated from each area of its business.

A. Go-Carts

_____

_____

B. Golf Driving Range

_____

_____

C. Batting Cages

_____

_____

D. Miniature Golf

_____

_____

Create a circle graph to illustrate the data.

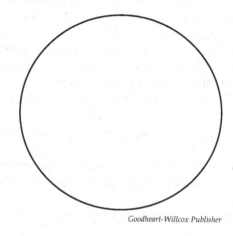

Goodheart-Willcox Publisher

5. Stop 'n Fuel is a highway rest stop that sells gasoline, food, and gifts. The following shows sales for five years from 2019 to 2023.
   - 2019: $400,000
   - 2020: $425,000
   - 2021: $465,000
   - 2022: $500,000
   - 2023: $550,000

The owner is planning for sales in 2024 to increase 10 percent over 2023 sales.

A. Calculate the planned sales for 2024.

_____

_____

B. Create a line graph to illustrate the actual sales from 2019 to 2023 and the planned sales for 2024. Indicate on your graph that the sales number for 2024 is an estimate.

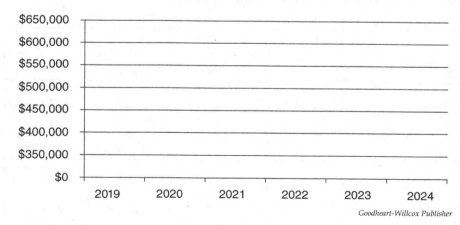

Goodheart-Willcox Publisher

Part 4: Communication Skills

Reading

All employees must read and comprehend company policies, often written in an employee handbook. Read the passage that follows and focus on the content. After you have read the passage, answer the questions that follow.

Dress Code

The DataSystems Computer Company requires all employees to present a professional image to the public, customers, prospective customers, and other business associates in order to ensure that those individuals are confident in our business integrity and competence. Accordingly, employees are required to wear appropriate business attire while at the office or any time they are conducting Company business. Although "business casual" attire is permitted, clothing that is too casual presents a poor image of the Company and is not allowed. Supervisors will offer guidance as to proper attire and are empowered to establish minimum standards for their employees that do not violate safety or health regulations. However, supervisors must be mindful of the Company's presentation to outsiders.

Here are some guidelines to be used by employees when selecting work attire, and by supervisors when setting standards for their department:

- Good grooming and proper personal hygiene are important. Employees should take care to ensure that their grooming and hygiene are not offensive to others.
- All employees are expected to wear business attire appropriate for the department in which they are assigned.
- Women should not wear any clothing that is too short, tight, or revealing. Midriff-bearing or low-cut garments are prohibited.
- Gentlemen should wear business suits or coordinating sport coats and slacks when greeting customers or vendors.
- Women should wear business-like dresses or coordinated skirt or pants outfits when greeting customers or vendors.
- Employees with visible tattoos may be asked to keep them covered while at work.
- Employees should wear business-type shoes.
- Employees are discouraged from wearing extremes in hairstyles, makeup, or jewelry, including body piercing.

Above all, employees should use common sense when selecting their wardrobe and reviewing their appearance. If in doubt about the appropriateness of a particular aspect of their appearance, employees should discuss the decision with their supervisor or the Human Resources Director.

The dress code applies to all employees, whether they are in customer contact positions or not. Exceptions to the dress code that must be made for certain health or other reasons must have the approval of the Human Resources Director. Employees who report for work in unacceptable attire or are inappropriately groomed may be sent home (without pay) in order to correct their appearance.

Reading Questions

1. What is the purpose of the dress code for this company?

   _____

   _____

   _____

   _____

   _____

   _____

2. Is business casual dress acceptable?

_____
_____
_____
_____
_____
_____

3. What should employees do if they are in doubt about the appropriateness of their appearance?

_____
_____
_____
_____
_____

Notes

Name _____ Date _____ Period _____

CHAPTER 22 Writing for Employment

Part 1: Content Review

Matching
Choose the letter of the correct term for each definition.

Terms:

A. résumé
B. reference
C. keyword
D. portfolio
E. job application

F. job interview
G. mock interview
H. employment verification
I. behavioral questions
J. background check

1. _____ A form with spaces for contact information, education, and work experience.

2. _____ A term that specifically relates to the functions of the position for which the employer is hiring.

3. _____ A document that profiles a person's career goals, education, and work history.

4. _____ The employer's opportunity to review a candidate's résumé and ask questions to see if the candidate is qualified for the position.

5. _____ A process through which the information provided on an applicant's résumé is checked to verify that it is correct.

6. _____ Questions that draw on an individual's previous experiences and decisions.

7. _____ A person who can comment on the qualifications, work ethic, personal qualities, and work-related aspects of another person's character.

8. _____ An investigation into personal data about a job applicant.

9. _____ A practice interview conducted with another person.

10. _____ A selection of related materials that an individual collects and organizes to show qualifications, skills, and talents to support a career or personal goal.

Multiple Choice
Choose the letter of the correct answer to each question.

1. _____ A résumé should include your _____.
   A. work experience
   B. Social Security number
   C. credit score
   D. All of the above.

2. _____ Which of the following is way to submit a résumé?
   A. In person
   B. By mail
   C. Online
   D. All of the above.

3. _____ When writing a résumé, a(n) _____ is a summary of the type of job for which the applicant is looking.
   A. portfolio
   B. reference
   C. career objective
   D. introduction

4. _____ The conclusion of a cover message should _____.
   A. provide a reference
   B. request an interview
   C. show your determination
   D. contain no keywords

5. _____ Which of the following is *not* a standard part of a résumé?
   A. Career objective
   B. Work experience
   C. Education
   D. Salary requirement

6. _____ The first step in preparing for a job interview is to learn as much as you can about _____.
   A. the job and the company
   B. company benefits
   C. the company dress code
   D. All of the above.

7. _____ Good telephone etiquette includes _____.
   A. introducing yourself
   B. stating the purpose of your call
   C. saying "please" and "thank you"
   D. All of the above.

8. _____ It is illegal for employers to ask job candidates about _____.
   A. hypothetical situations
   B. salary requirements
   C. their religion
   D. their education

9. _____ A prospective employer asks you to describe a situation when you made a mistake. This is an example of a(n) _____ question.
   A. behavioral
   B. hypothetical
   C. empathetic
   D. illegal

10. _____ After a job interview, a job candidate should immediately write a(n) _____.
    A. updated résumé
    B. thank-you message
    C. cover message
    D. Form W-4

Completion

Choose the word(s) that best completes each of the following statements.

1. The _____ section of a résumé includes details about an individual's work history.

_____

2. A(n) _____ résumé lists information in reverse chronological order, with the most recent employer listed first.

_____

3. The _____ of a cover message should demonstrate your positive work behaviors and qualities that make you employable.

_____

4. A practice interview conducted with another person is a(n) _____.

_____

5. Speaking words to communicate is _____ communication.

_____

6. _____ questions require candidates to imagine a situation and describe how they would act.

_____

7. _____ questions draw on an individual's previous experiences and decisions.

_____

8. After a job interview, _____ your performance so that you improve for the next interview.

_____

9. A(n) _____ is used to verify an employee's identity and that the individual is authorized to work in the United States.

_____

10. A(n) _____ provides an employer with the information necessary to withhold the appropriate amount of taxes from an employee's paycheck.

_____

Part 2: Concept Review

Open Response

Respond to each of the following statements or questions. Use complete sentences.

1. What is a cover message? Why should a job applicant write one?

   _____

   _____

   _____

   _____

   _____

   _____

2. List four possible sources of information to learn about a company prior to a job interview.

   _____

   _____

   _____

   _____

   _____

   _____

3. Imagine you went on a job interview but discovered that you were not interested in the job. Explain why the interview was not a waste of time.

   _____

   _____

   _____

   _____

   _____

   _____

4. Why can the employment process take a substantial amount of time?

   _____

   _____

   _____

   _____

   _____

   _____

Name _____

5. You are applying for a sales associate position in a retail store that sells casual apparel for young men and women. Make a list of five questions you would like to ask the interviewer about the company, position, responsibilities, etc.

_____

_____

_____

_____

_____

_____

_____

_____

Part 3: Math Skills

Ratios

Many businesses calculate ratios to help analyze their performance. A *ratio* is a mathematical measure that compares two numbers through division. Ratios are often expressed as a fraction. For example, a drugstore sells a bottle of shampoo for $4 which cost the store $3. The ratio of the selling price to the cost can be expressed as $4 ÷ $3 = 4/3.

Answer the following problems involving ratios.

1. Reynolds Drugstore sells three different brands of vitamin C tablets in 100-count bottles. Calculate the ratio of selling price to cost for each of the following brands. Which brand has the highest selling price ratio?

   A. Nutri-Best

   Selling Price: $12.99

   Cost: $7.50

   _____

   _____

   B. Vita-Man

   Selling Price: $15.99

   Cost: $8.75

   _____

   _____

   C. Reynolds Private Label

   Selling Price: $9.99

   Cost: $4.25

   _____

   _____

   _____

2. Adventure Industries manufactures all-terrain vehicles (ATVs). The company started a promotion offering a $1,000 rebate on three of its ATV models. Calculate the ratio of the rebate to the list price of the following ATVs. Determine which model has the biggest percentage discount.

   A. Sidewinder X200: List price: $8,300

   _____

   _____

   B. Sidewinder X400: List price: $6,000

   _____

   _____

   C. Sidewinder X600: List price: $4,900

   _____

   _____

   _____

Name _____

3. Inventory turnover is a ratio which tells how often a business' inventory is sold and replaced over a time period. The formula for the turnover ratio is

$$\frac{\text{cost of goods sold}}{\text{average inventory}} = \text{turnover rate}$$

Big Dollar Stores sold merchandise at its stores last year that cost $1,700,000. The average value of the inventory in its stores was $500,000. Calculate Big Dollar's turnover rate and determine how many times its inventory was sold and replaced.

_____

_____

4. Big Dollar Stores has two departments: Food and Household Supplies. Calculate the turnover rate for each department based on the following figures. Which department had the higher turnover rate?

A. Food

Average inventory: $225,000

Cost of goods sold: $1,100,000

_____

_____

B. Household Supplies

Average inventory: $275,000

Cost of goods sold: $600,000

_____

_____

5. Return on equity is a ratio that measures the rate of return the owner is earning on personal investment in the business. The formula for return on equity is

$$\frac{\text{Net Income}}{\text{Owner's Equity}} = \text{Return on Equity}$$

Martin opens an antiques store with a $200,000 equity investment. Last year, Martin earned a net income of $20,000. Martin's rate of return on the equity investment is:

$$\frac{\$20,000}{\$200,000} = .10 = 10\%$$

Leslie made a $150,000 equity investment in a business that develops tax preparation software. Last year, the business earned a net income of $36,000. What is Leslie's rate of return on the equity investment?

_____

_____

Part 4: Communication Skills

Writing

Read the following qualifications. Imagine you have achieved these things and are looking for a job to fit your experience.

- Received a bachelor's degree in marketing
- Worked for another publisher for three years
- Looking for a position with more opportunities and challenges
- Experienced in the education sales market
- Accustomed to travel
- Self-starter

Now, read the following job description.

Outside Sales Representative

Publishers, Inc. seeks a career-oriented salesperson to work the North Carolina, South Carolina, and Georgia territory. Previous technical, teaching, and/or sales experience preferred. Travel required. The candidate will work independently in their territory while maintaining close contact with management. Some responsibilities include the following:

- Travel to make sales calls to teachers and administrators in middle schools, high schools, career and technical schools, community colleges, private training schools, and four-year colleges and universities.
- Attend state and local career and technical, family and consumer sciences, technology, and trade and industrial conventions and/or in-service workshops within the assigned territory.
- Communicate regularly with the National Sales Manager to provide information on customers, specific issues, sales, product information, and general economic and business issues.
- Provide product and market feedback to our in-house staff to be used when revising existing product and developing new product.

Requirements Include:

- Bachelor's degree
- Strong leadership, communication, and group presentation skills
- Microsoft Office program skills
- Sales experience preferred
- Must be well-organized, self-motivated, and highly energetic

To apply for this position, please e-mail your cover letter and résumé to publishers@email.com.

Craft a message that you would put in an e-mail to apply for the position.

_____

_____

_____

_____

_____

_____

_____

_____

_____

_____

_____

_____

CHAPTER 23 Digital Citizenship

Part 1: Content Review

Matching

Choose the letter of the correct term for each definition.

Terms:

A. digital communication

B. digital literacy

C. digital footprint

D. piracy

E. public domain

F. authentication

G. hacking

H. cookies

I. spyware

J. firewall

1. _____ The unethical and illegal copying or downloading of software, files, and other protected material.

2. _____ The process of verifying a user's identity.

3. _____ The exchange of information through electronic means.

4. _____ The ability to use technology to locate, evaluate, communicate, and create information.

5. _____ Software that spies on a computer.

6. _____ A program that monitors information coming into a computer.

7. _____ Material that is not owned by anybody and can be used without permission.

8. _____ Illegally accessing or altering digital devices, software, or networks.

9. _____ A data record of all an individual's online activities.

10. _____ Bits of data stored on your computer that record information about the websites you have visited.

Multiple Choice

Choose the letter of the correct answer to each question.

1. _____ Using the Internet to harass or threaten an individual is _____.
   A. plagiarism
   B. hacking
   C. cyberbullying
   D. spamming

2. _____ _____ is sending unwanted mass e-mails or intentionally flooding an individual's social media site or e-mail inbox with unwanted messages.
   A. Plagiarism
   B. Hacking
   C. Cyberbullying
   D. Spamming

3. _____ Crimes of defamation are _____.
   A. slander and libel
   B. flaming and spamming
   C. plagiarism and piracy
   D. infringement and phishing

4. _____ Which of the following protects intellectual property?
   A. Copyright
   B. Patent
   C. Trademark
   D. All of the above.

5. _____ The legal permission to use a software program is a _____.
   A. patent
   B. license
   C. trademark
   D. All of the above.

6. _____ A set of rules concerning the use of company-owned and company-operated equipment is found in a(n) _____.
   A. Electronic User's Bill of Rights
   B. acceptable use policy
   C. Internet protocol address
   D. General Public License

7. _____ The use of fraudulent e-mails and copies of valid websites to trick people into providing private and confidential data is _____.
   A. phishing
   B. hacking
   C. piracy
   D. infringement

8. _____ Which of the following is *not* a form of malware?
   A. Spyware
   B. Cookies
   C. Worms
   D. Trojan horse

9. _____ An illegal act that involves stealing someone's personal information and using that information to commit theft or fraud is _____.
   A. phishing
   B. hacking
   C. identify theft
   D. defamation

10. _____ Companies and schools can use _____ to prevent unauthorized Internet surfing or visiting selected websites during working hours.
    A. pop-up blockers
    B. firewalls
    C. filters
    D. regular backups

Completion

Choose the word(s) that best completes each of the following statements.

1. Someone who regularly and skillfully engages in the use of technology, such as the Internet, computers, and other digital devices, is a(n) _____.

2. The standard of appropriate behavior when using technology to communicate is ____.

_____

3. The art of using good manners in any situation is ____.

_____

4. Something that comes from a person's mind, such as an idea, invention, or process, is considered ____.

_____

5. The unethical and illegal practice of claiming another person's material as your own is ____.

_____

6. Many websites list rules, called the ____, which must be followed for downloaded files.

_____

7. ____ is the use of multiple authentication techniques to verify a person's identity.

_____

8. ____ is a term that refers to software programs that are intended to damage, destroy, or steal data.

_____

9. ____ are malware usually disguised to appear as a useful or common application in order to convince people to download or use the program.

_____

10. A computer program designed to negatively impact a computer system by infecting other files is a(n) ____.

_____

Part 2: Concept Review

Open Response

Respond to each of the following statements or questions. Use complete sentences.

1. What is a digital footprint? How does this apply to social media sites and e-mail?

_____

_____

_____

_____

_____

_____

_____

2. What is a copyright? Do copyright rules apply to information on the Internet?

_____

_____

_____

_____

_____

3. Explain the risk of using public Wi-Fi hotspots.

_____

_____

_____

_____

_____

4. What does it mean to "back up" your computer? Why is this important?

_____

_____

_____

_____

_____

_____

5. You are helping to establish policies for your company regarding the proper use of computers by employees. Make a list of five instructions you would give employees to help protect your company's time, property, and digital security.

_____

_____

_____

_____

_____

_____

_____

_____

_____

_____

Part 3: Math Skills

Percentages

Basic math skills are needed in both business planning and personal management. The ability to calculate percentages is a useful skill in planning business sales, goals, and personal budgets. To find the percentage of a number, change the percentage to a decimal by moving the decimal point two places to the left. Then, multiply the decimal by the number.

Answer the following questions about percentages.

1. King Computer Specialties is an online retailer of computer accessories. Sales in February last year were $47,000. The company is planning for sales this February to be 10 percent higher than last year. The formula for the planned increase is:

   past sales × percentage increase = planned increase

   The formula for planned sales is:

   past sales + planned increase = planned sales

   For King Computer Specialties, calculate the planned increase and planned sales for this February.

   _____

   _____

   _____

2. Rayburn Optics had $200,000 in sales last year. This year the company will introduce new products and plans for a 15 percent increase in sales. Calculate the planned increase and planned sales for this year.

   _____

   _____

   _____

3. Keweenaw Jam Pot makes and sells a variety of fruit jellies and jams in the Upper Peninsula of Michigan. This business is highly seasonal. In fact, the store is only open during the warm-weather tourist season, which runs from May through August. Last year sales were as follows:
   • May: $15,000
   • June: $20,000
   • July: $29,000
   • August: $33,000

   Keweenaw Jam Pot plans on a 6 percent sales increase each month over last year. Determine the planned increase and sales for each month this year. Then, calculate the planned sales for the entire four-month season.

   A. Last year sales for May = $15,000

   planned increase = _____

   _____

   _____

   planned sales = _____

   _____

   _____

   B. Last year sales for June = $20,000

   planned increase = _____

   _____

   _____

planned sales = _____

_____

_____

C. Last year sales for July = $29,000

planned increase = _____

_____

_____

planned sales = _____

_____

_____

D. Last year sales for August = $33,000

planned increase = _____

_____

_____

planned sales = _____

_____

_____

E. Planned sales for four-month season =

_____

_____

4. It is February and Keweenaw Jam Pot is planning its inventory for the coming tourist season. Last year, there was $60,000 in retail stock at the beginning of May. In May of this year, the company plans to have an additional 6 percent over last year.

A. How much should inventory be increased over last year?

_____

_____

B. How much inventory should be on hand in May of this year?

_____

_____

5. Patty's Party Center is a retailer that sells party supplies and giftware. A vendor offers a line of fall decorations and tableware with a special 5 percent seasonal discount. Patty's Party Center places a $3,800 order. Calculate the discount and invoice amount using the following formulas:

order amount × discount percentage = discount amount

order amount − discount = invoice amount

_____

_____

_____

Part 4: Communication Skills

Reading

Employee handbooks often have policies regarding business communications, especially e-mail communication. Read the passage below and focus on the content. After you have read the passage, answer the questions that follow.

E-mail Policy

- **Communicating information:** Content of all communications should be professional and accurate. Users should use the same care in drafting e-mail and other electronic documents as they would for any other written communication. Anything created on the computer may, and likely will, be reviewed by others.
- **E-mail retention:** Unless directed by your supervisor, employees should discard inactive e-mail after sixty (60) days.
- **E-mail subscription lists:** Users may not use their assigned Company e-mail address to join e-mail subscription lists that are non-job related. Users may join e-mail subscription lists using their assigned Company e-mail address only when the subscription is job related.
- **Sending unsolicited e-mail ("spamming"):** Without the express permission of their supervisor, users may not send unsolicited e-mail to persons with whom they do not have a prior relationship. Users may not, under any circumstances, attempt to disguise their identities in sending electronic communications.
- **Solicitation and personal e-mail:** Under no circumstances should the Company's e-mail system be used for solicitation. Employees should refrain from using the Company e-mail to correspond with others outside the Company except where necessary to conduct the Company's business. Under no circumstances should an employee open an e-mail or an e-mail attachment from any unknown source.

Reading Questions

1. How long should inactive e-mail be kept?

_____

_____

_____

_____

2. Is it permissible for an employee to use a company e-mail address for subscription lists?

_____

_____

_____

_____

3. Are employees allowed to send unsolicited e-mail?

_____

_____

_____

_____